PROJECT LEARNING

for the

MULTIPLE INTELLIGENCES

CLASSROOM

Sally Berman

SkyLight
TRAINING AND PUBLISHING, INC.
Arlington Heights, Illinois

371.36
B516

Project Learning for the Multiple Intelligences Classroom

Published by SkyLight Training and Publishing, Inc.
2626 S. Clearbrook Dr., Arlington Heights, IL 60005
800-348-4474 or 847-290-6600
FAX 847-290-6609
info@iriskylight.com
http://www.iriskylight.com

Creative Director: Robin Fogarty
Managing Editor: Ela Aktay
Editor: Sue Schumer
Proofreader: Amy Kinsman
Graphic Designer: Heidi Ray
Cover and Illustration Designer: David Stockman
Production Supervisor: Bob Crump

LCCCN 97-77116
ISBN 1-57517-077-9

2090-10-97V
Item Number 1571
06 05 04 03 02 01 00 99 98 97   15 14 13 12 11 10 9 8 7 6 5 4 3 2 1

To Al,
my partner in projects, and
to Lois,
my partner in brainstorming

Contents

SkyLight Training and Publishing, Inc.

Foreword

Do not then train youths to learn by force and harshness, but direct them to it by what amuses their minds so that you may be better able to discover with accuracy the peculiar bent of the genius of each.

—Plato

With the advent of multiple intelligences theory, emergent brain research and the case for coherent, connected-curriculum, and performance-based assessments, project learning becomes paramount as a pedagogical architecture.

Through brain imaging technologies alone, the data are clear and unmistakable. Brain activity increases as the learner puzzles over problematic situations. Electrical impulses result from the complex sensory input caused by wonderment and challenge and this electrical activity ignites the neurons in the brain. Neural pathways are created as the brain actually "grows dendrites" for interconnectivity between brain cells. Thus, problem solving does, in fact, "grow intelligence."

If this is true, and the evidence is pretty convincing that it is, then the mission of schooling becomes clear. The mission of school is to "grow the intelligence" of each human being in its care. And, if this "intelligence growing" is done best through complex, compelling activities that engage the learner intellectually, project learning as a third-generation model of authentic integrated instruction is a viable option.

Think about project-based learning for a minute from these perspectives. Have you started to clean out the garage and found yourself immersed in the project? Or started weeding the garden and realized that several hours had passed? Have you ever entered a kite-flying contest and worked late into the night preparing the perfect kite for entry in the next day's event? Or started a scrapbook or photo album—sorting, arranging, rearranging, pasting, and labeling for hours at a time? If you are nodding your head "yes" in answer to these questions, you know how absolutely engaging projects can be for the mind and body of the participant.

In *Project Learning for the Multiple Intelligences Classroom*, Sally Berman develops projects in a way that demonstrates the versatility of projects across subject areas and for learners of any age. Ranging across the spectrum from building bird feeders to redesigning the shopping cart, these projects draw students into problem solving. Learners are bound to "sprout dendrites" at an unprecedented rate! As they ponder and puzzle, and their projects take shape, students will truly be making new connections in their brains. These learners will be reviving their neural networks in ways that increase their capacity for problem solving and decision making. They will become more intelligent. With that in mind—bring on the projects!

—Robin Fogarty

SkyLight Training and Publishing, Inc.

Acknowledgments

Robin Fogarty "made me" write this book. She began by asking me to brain-storm some project ideas, then asked if I could write up a few, and the next thing I knew, I was saying, "Oh, yes, I can do a book on that!" Sue Schumer, editor for this project on projects, polished text, asked key clarifying questions, provided information and suggestions, and shared in the creative dialogue. The kids I taught, mostly eleventh graders, did many of these projects. Because of their eager performances, I can guarantee that kids will do even the seemingly silly, "hokey," parts of the projects and love doing them. Kids really do like to be silly as long as they are told that it is all right to lighten up and have fun. The North Woods gave my brain room to roam as I played with these project ideas and the big lake helped me remember that dead calm does not necessarily mean brain dead—it might be the build up for the next brainstorm. Oliver Wendell Holmes gave me the big picture, so, remembering his words, I opened up my skylights and let the learning projects take form. I hope that readers will enjoy using them as much as I enjoyed writing them.

Introduction

Project learning engages students in creating, testing, polishing, and producing something. An observable indicator that students have completed a project is a tangible, student-produced object such as a book, a script, or an invention. Students go into the project with the end-product in mind. They know from the outset that they have a specific amount of time—a week, a month, a quarter, or a semester—to complete the product. They know the project guidelines and how the final product will be evaluated before they begin working. This knowledge helps them to self-evaluate as they do the project. They know the target toward which they are working, so they can analyze, refine, discard, polish, and shape the product as they go. They may do a performance or make a presentation or demonstration as a final project activity—it is a presentation or performance of their own product. The student-made object is the key to distinguishing between project learning and performance or presentation learning.

This is hands-on learning at its best; the result is authentic, lifelong learning. When a group of thirty-somethings were asked to tell what they remembered the best about their middle school years, one individual said, "I remember doing a project about African ants. We did a diorama of African anthills, made puppets of the ants, wrote a script for a puppet show, and presented the puppet show when I was in the fourth grade. I still remember most of what we learned about African ants as we did the project." Another person added, "When I was in the fifth grade, the teacher divided the class into small groups and had each group do a project about some wonder of an ancient civilization. My group did the pyramids and sphinx that are near modern Cairo, Egypt. We constructed the pyramids so that they opened and we could show hidden passages and chambers. We furnished and decorated the chambers to represent the burial chambers of Egyptian nobility. I don't remember much of the rest of fifth grade. I suppose I remember the pyramids so well because we did them as a project." A third person said, "When I was in the fifth grade, some friends and I wrote a play about the Wright brothers. The teacher had said that each group in the class was to do a play about some American inventor and the impact of a particular invention on our lives. We asked if we could do Orville and Wilbur Wright as one inventor because they worked together. The teacher liked the play so well that she let us present it to the whole school during an assembly—I still remember many of the details of that play." In each case, individuals remembered best what they had learned actively. As they collected and sorted through information, decided what to keep and what to discard, redesigned and refined the final product, and, ultimately, celebrated success, they acquired information that stuck with them.

Students learn how to learn as they do projects. They become more skillful information collectors and organizers. They learn how to analyze information to decide whether it is useful. They develop more skillful questioning techniques and discover that getting the right information is often a matter of asking the right question. They become less defensive when critiqued as they learn how to evaluate their own work and look for ways to improve their products. They discover the joy of celebrating success. And they realize that doing effective learning involves being willing to take risks, make mistakes, become confused, and learn with and from others.

PROJECT CATEGORIES

Guidelines for projects do not all look and sound alike. Some projects have very tight parameters. Others point students in a general direction and then give them lots of freedom. This book includes five kinds of projects: structured, topic-related, genre-related, template, and open-ended projects. A single project may combine two of these types. Some projects simply seem to be difficult to categorize. The following descriptions may serve as a springboard for the creation of projects as well as a way to classify them.

Structured Projects

Structured projects ask for products that fit very specific guidelines. Students are told that their product must be a certain size, contain specific materials or parts, be able to perform a specific job or function, and meet defined quality standards. Students are given a set amount of time to make the product—a week, a month, a quarter, or a semester. They are asked to demonstrate the completed products to show that these products meet the guidelines. Products that fulfill the specifications are rated successful. Those that cannot do the job or meet the quality standards are disqualified.

One of the best-known structured projects, one familiar to many science teachers, is the Egg Drop. In this project, students are asked to design a container that will keep a raw egg from breaking when container and egg are dropped from a height of six feet. They are told that the container may be made of any material and filled with any cushioning of their choice so long as the combined weight of egg, container, and cushioning does not exceed a specified total (perhaps 500 grams). Students are also told that the container may have maximum dimensions, thirty centimeters per side for example. Students are given a limited amount of time to design and test the product and bring it to class. On the due date, all Egg Drop containers are tested. If a container and egg make it through the drop intact, the container is labeled "professional." If the container breaks but the egg does not, the container is labeled "redesign." If the container and egg both break, the container is labeled "disqualified."

When students do structured projects such as the Egg Drop, they make working objects that function identically. Genre-related and template projects, on the other hand, may involve products that are similar in materials, appearance, and size that do not necessarily do the same job. The products of a structured project all do the same job. In the Egg Drop, they all keep the egg from breaking.

In another familiar science project, the Catapult, students are required to construct catapults that all hurl identical objects the same distance, say sixty feet. The Bridge Building project requires students to build bridges using craft sticks. All of the bridges must be the same length and height and must be able to support the same weight for a given length of time. Many science Olympiad projects are such structured projects.

Topic-Related Projects

Topic-related projects extend student learning from a unit of study. These are the projects that most people think of when they hear the phrase "project learning." Students pick a project topic from a teacher- or student-made list of options, or the teacher may assign the topics. Each student gathers information about her topic, analyzes, sorts and combines the information, and crafts a final product. This final product often is a written report that tells what she has learned and what personal meaning it has for her and a presentation product that may include the use of slides, video or audio tapes, posters, pamphlets or magazines, or other audio and visual aids. If topic-related projects are assigned to small groups, the groups do joint written reports that describe their learning and collaborate on presenting the project to the class. The written reports and presentation tools are displayed in the classroom for a time.

As a student gathers information about her topic, she often develops a deeper interest in the topic and a more complete understanding of the personal meaning that it has for her. She would begin the project by choosing her topic. For example, a student studying the Great Lakes might select a topic from a list of specific geological features like Niagara Falls, the straits of Mackinac, or Isle Royale; natural resources like lumber, copper, and amethyst; cities like Cleveland, Detroit, Duluth, or Thunder Bay; explorers like Radisson and Groseilliers, Jacques Marquette, or Douglas Houghton; or industries like shipping, steel-making, and plastics manufacturing. If a student selects Duluth as her topic, she might write and produce a videotaped commercial promoting tourism to that city and produce a magazine with articles that showcase the Duluth lifestyle. A completed project on a natural resource such as amethyst might feature a storyboard showing the source as well as extraction and use of that resource; a brochure describing the impact of amethyst-mining and shipping on the local economy; and a journal in which she imagines that she is an eyewitness to events that occur when the nonrenewable resource is gone and the mines close.

Topic-related projects involve many students or groups of students doing separate projects that all connect to a single, larger unit of study. Everyone in the class experiences expanded learning about the unit of study when the projects are completed and the products are presented to the class. These projects are often assigned early in the unit. As the unit progresses, students are encouraged to report the progress that they have made toward completion of the project to the teacher or another student—a "project buddy." If the projects are being done by small groups of students, the teacher may want to schedule in-class time for the groups to coordinate work on the projects and report their progress to the teacher. Individuals or small groups present the finished products to the whole class at the end of the unit. The display of finished products allows everyone to review the extended learning for some time after the class has moved on to other units of study.

Genre-Related Projects

A genre-related project asks students to fashion a product of a certain kind or sort or type, containing certain critical elements for which there are clear parameters. Students use the parameters as guidelines when they create their products. Students are encouraged to use some creativity in designing the final product. The teacher may give students the project guidelines or lead a class meeting in which students brainstorm the critical elements and their parameters.

For example, if the genre is children's literature, students may decide that a storybook has front and back covers, a title page, and pages that combine story and pictures. For each of these critical elements, students can then brainstorm the "publishing house" standards. They may find this easier to do if they have samples of published storybooks to look at as they describe these parameters. The teacher and students can use ideas from the brainstorm to develop a rubric that students can use to self evaluate their storybooks during development. The rubric can describe a storybook of professional quality, one that is a work in progress, and a storybook that is a rough draft. A column for "missing and not forgotten" elements is very helpful when students are self-evaluating their products.

Other genre-related projects could ask students to produce other forms of literature like biographies or plays, types of performances like monster movies or infomercials, kinds of music like country or rap, and forms of recreation like board games. For example, a biology teacher may ask students to do a genre-related project in which they create board games that show the repopulation of an area that has been devastated by a natural disaster like the eruption of a volcano or a flood.

In such a project, the teacher may ask her students to bring in board games from home so that the class can examine professionally manufactured games and then brainstorm the critical elements and the parameters they have in common. After the class has finished the brainstorm, the teacher can give the class any additional information she feels they need—she may set a due date, suggest target dates for different stages of completion, and tell students how they will submit or present the final products. Students may then produce their board games complete with playing instructions and present the games by having their classmates play the games. Different individuals or groups may devise board games that have different layouts—Monopoly, for example, has a very different layout from Trivial Pursuit—while retaining the same critical elements such as a clear start and finish, differently designed game tokens for different players, some way to determine how many spaces to move in a turn, some way to decide when a player's turn is "up," and, perhaps, some forms of penalties to move players backward. It is the "different surface look with same critical elements" nature of these projects that defines them as genre-related rather than structured or template projects.

Template Projects

Template projects are built on tailor-made material. The generally accepted form, pattern, or structure for the material suggests the uses to which the template can be put. Field guides, for example, follow the same general template. Whether students look at Peterson's *Wildflowers,* Brockman's *Trees of North America,* or Pough's *Audubon Water Bird Guide,* or other standard field guides, they will see the information organized in almost identical ways. The users of field guides expect a certain structure, and the authors follow that expected template.

Newspapers also follow a generally accepted structure. Whether they are major city dailies or small town weeklies, newspapers begin with "hard" news stories of local interest, continue with national and international news, then go to editorials, letters from readers, commentary, features, and sports. Students can use this template to create a classroom or school newspaper, to write a newspaper for a given historical event like the Battle of Shiloh, or to write a "newspaper of the not-yet" in which they imagine events 100 years in the future.

The top ten list as popularized by talk-show host David Letterman is a template for prioritizing information or ideas. "The top ten reasons for—" lists now appear in newspapers, magazines, and on the Internet for a wide variety of topics. The lists are always presented in the same way. They are titled, begin with reason number ten, end with "and the number one reason for—is—," and use humor to make the point. Although the form is always the same, the content can focus on almost any topic. Within the generally accepted structure, students can be creative. This is true of all template projects. The final product has a recognizable look because of the template, and the final product has a unique look because of the individuality of its creators.

Open-Ended Projects

Open-ended projects encourage risk-taking, creativity, and innovative and divergent thinking. Students begin these projects with minimal guidelines and few criteria. Students may find themselves looking at familiar objects from a new point of view or examining familiar materials to find new applications. The teacher and students set up the projects by discussing the guidelines which might include suggested due dates for collecting information, brainstorming ideas, testing products, and completing final products. Teachers may also want to tell students that many of our everyday materials and inventions resulted from individuals working on open-ended projects. Recycled landscaping timbers which are made of plastic from milk and laundry product bottles were created by engineers who were challenged by their employers to invent processes and products that would keep these plastics out of landfills. Deja Shoes were invented by a woman from California who wanted to find uses for scrap tires.

Students may design and build a prototype that will (probably) never see mass production. They may be asked, for example, to build an all-terrain vehicle from alternative transportation, like skateboards. They may be asked to develop all-weather housing from common kitchen products. Or they may be asked to redesign and rebuild a household item for a different segment of the population—to make a potato peeler or egg beater that can be used by five year olds or a needle that can be threaded by eighty-five year olds who have lost their glasses. The open-endedness of the project takes them into new territory where they are free to visualize, create, and invent. Open-ended projects work well for encouraging creativity in small groups of students. The lack of structure of these projects invites productive brainstorming in the groups.

THE DEVELOPMENT OF A PROJECT

Regardless of project type, all projects begin, develop, and mature using a cycle of defining, selecting the project, reading, listening, searching, gathering information, analyzing, sketching, organizing, including, discarding, model-making, regathering, revising, revamping, reconstruction, testing, evaluating, including, discarding, more gathering—until the final product is done and tested and then evaluated and measured for improvement. Oliver Wendell Holmes said:

> There are one-story intellects,
> two-story intellects,
> three-story intellects with skylights.
> All fact-collectors,
> who have no aim beyond their facts,
> are one-story men.

Two-story men compare, reason, generalize,
using the labor of fact collectors as their own.
Three-story men idealize, imagine, predict;
Their best illumination comes from above, through the
skylight.

When students do projects, the three stories are not sequential. Students move back and forth between levels, gathering information, processing and regathering, applying and reprocessing, and reapplying and regathering. The process of completing a project can be wonderfully messy. Teachers and students may find the Holmes quote useful because it may help them remember that thoughtful projects that result in authentic learning involve activities at all three levels. Information needs to be gathered carefully from a variety of sources, analyzed and recombined to form new ideas, and incorporated into a final product.

The First-Story Intellect: Gathering Activities

Students select projects or the teacher assigns projects. The teacher and the students discuss guidelines and time lines. Then the students begin to read, research, interview, and gather facts. Students take care to gather information carefully. They know that later success depends on doing careful groundwork now. Students find resources, use references, and do many of the activities listed below.

Gathering Ideas: Researching the Project

Reading for background information

Researching and taking notes

Building a reference list

Interviewing experts

Viewing films and videos

Developing an outline

Talking with peers

Surfing the Internet

Checking and double-checking sources

Visiting sites

Gathering charts, maps, illustrations

As students begin to perceive that the information is beginning to suggest a product, they move into the second story.

The Second-Story Intellect: Processing Activities

Now students begin to immerse themselves in their information. Their minds try to analyze the information, create meaningful chunks of information, and synthesize the information to form new ideas and finalize the product. Team members gather to trade information and discard duplications. As students reorganize and sort information into meaningful chunks, they may discover that some information seems incorrect or incomplete. The teacher may hear that, "Johnny isn't doing his share of the work." An individual or group may be able to move ahead independently. They may also need some guidance from the teacher. They may need to hear that it's OK for them to take a fresh look at what they have and where they planned to go and to revise their ideas or replan their product. This reorganization can lead to renewed efforts and a higher level of creativity in the final product. As students work to make sense of information and reorganize, they will do many of the actions in the following list.

Processing Information: Crystallizing Ideas

Brainstorming ideas	Reconciling conflicting data
Analyzing data	Finding a focus
Charting information	Assigning a theme
Drawing and sketching models	Creating a metaphor
Drafting ideas	Looking for patterns
Developing prototypes	Seeking connections
Filling in missing information	Playing with ideas
Visualizing the big picture	Finding materials

At this time, students will also begin to "run between floors." They will go back to the first story to gather new information, and they will run up to the third story to begin work on the final product.

The Third-Story Intellect: Applying Ideas

Once students begin to assemble the final product, work accelerates. They sense that the end is near and they are eager to get to the final product. There may be some trips back to the first floor for extra information and some tugging at ideas to get the right fit. Students constantly self evaluate the product as it takes shape to revise, reinvent, restructure, and improve. They want to make the best product that they can. As they finish the project, students will do some of these things.

SkyLight Training and Publishing, Inc.

Applying Ideas: Trying and Testing

Model building	Evaluative testing
Construction	Peer review
Assembling	Self-assessment
Synthesizing ideas	Evaluation against criteria
Rethinking or reconceptualizing	Expert review
Finishing touches	Final submittals
Decorative details	Celebrations

USING THIS BOOK

Readers are encouraged to keep the following points in mind as they read this book.

First, the nine projects in this book fit into three categories: basic, intermediate, and advanced. Each project has been flexibly designed so that it can be used with elementary school, middle school, or high school students. A teacher may want to use a project exactly as it is written or the individual may want to tailor the project to fit his or her students more precisely.

Second, the end of each chapter includes project-learning logs and a project rubric, which may be reproduced for classroom purposes. The learning log is divided into three parts—gathering, processing, and applying—to encourage students to review their learning strategies after each phase of the project. Students may use the rubric for ongoing self-evaluation as they do the project; they may compare what they have done with the indicators in the rubric to decide what about their work is strong and what they want to strengthen or revise. At the end of the project, students and teachers can use this rubric to determine a final project grade.

Third, the appendix of this book contains blackline masters that list learning strategies. These strategies target multiple intelligences for each stage of the three-story intellect. Using the three-story intellect model moves learners from the concrete to the abstract as they do a project. Including strategies that target all intelligences allows all learners to work in their personal comfort zones at least part of the time. Teachers are encouraged to use these blackline masters as they develop their own project plans.

Fourth, during the final phase of a project, each student processes cognitively and metacognitively by doing a self-assessment journal entry in which he or she highlights content learning from the project, analyzes multiple intelligence comfort levels, identifies and evaluates thinking strategies, assesses his or her effectiveness as a member of a learning team, and plans strategies. These journal entries provide a record of learning, thinking, and growing that the student experienced while doing the project.

Finally, the teacher is encouraged to use the projects in this book as catalysts for developing his or her own projects and using them to help students enhance their learning. Project learning works because it is student-centered, active, hands-on learning. As students experience the freedom to gather information and organize it themselves, they also experience the power of being capable, competent learners. As they self-evaluate, they experience the joy of giving themselves credit for a job well done and the realization that any product can be improved. Project learning works because it empowers learners and encourages them to want to learn more. Teachers and students will find that doing three-story intellect projects will help them become partners in lifelong learning.

PART I

BASIC PROJECTS

Chapter 1

What a Wonderful State!

A Social Studies Project

This project focuses students' attention on a particular state within the United States. Appropriate for those students who are being introduced to geography, this project is based on the assumption that they have just begun to learn the relative locations of regions, states, cities, land forms, natural resources, and bodies of water and to investigate the interactions of people and the land and plants and animals with each other. These students are starting to use maps as well as atlases, globes, and other resources to gather information about the planet. Through this project, "What a Wonderful State!", they will acquire knowledge related to geography and social studies and develop fundamental skills in the context of project learning in the multiple intelligences classroom.

As students begin this project, the teacher will need to decide whether to have them work individually or in groups of three. The teacher may make the group assignments or allow the students to organize themselves in groups. Suggested roles with the groups are a researcher who keeps the team on task as well on time and uses reference material to double-check ideas for accuracy; an illustrator who does pencil sketches of ideas for the final group product and encourages everyone to participate; and a calligrapher who does the lettering for the group product and checks for agreement and ranking of ideas for the final product. All three group members will play an active part in presenting the finished project to the class.

Students may choose the states that they want to study or the teacher may assign a "target" state to each group of students. Each group will *gather* information about a different state by reading, listening, investigating resources, and compiling a list of findings.

The student groups will need to *process* information and eventually come up with a list of ten information pieces about the state—facts or features they find the most meaningful or interesting. Each group will teach the rest of the class about the target state by presenting their project—the top ten

list in its completed form. At the conclusion of the project, the various groups will arrange a display of all their top ten lists according to their relative locations in the United States, going from west to east and south to north. The teacher may want to distribute the project evaluation rubric (page 23) at the beginning of the project, so students will know the evaluation criteria.

This activity is an example of a *template project.* Groups develop their top ten lists using the pattern or structure of the top ten list that David Letterman has popularized on his *Late Night* television program. Letterman starts reading the list from the bottom, beginning with number ten. For the "What a Wonderful State!" project, the title of the list is "The Top Ten Reasons Why We Love (name of state)." Each group will use the completed top ten list to tell in words and show in pictures its favorite ten information pieces about the targeted state. Students will verify the accuracy of the facts or features they include in the list.

✴ FIRST-STORY INTELLECT

Gathering Information

Groups use first-story intellect activities to begin gathering information. (Refer to Project Learning Log 1 at the end of the chapter.) Students may read information about their state in resource materials such as atlases, encyclopedias, and social studies text books. They may choose to read a story book that contains information and pictures about the target state. For example, a group that has chosen Michigan as the target state may decide to read *Paddle-to-the-Sea* (Holling 1941). The book describes the adventures of a small wooden canoe that an Indian boy carves and places in the snowpack on a hilltop north of Lake Superior. The canoe is carried by melting snow into a stream; the stream sweeps it into a river; the river washes it into Lake Superior; and eventually the carved canoe finds its way to the ocean. As the canoe floats along the Michigan shore line and, at times, is carried overland, the author identifies some of the natural resources found in Michigan—such as copper and timber, some natural features—such as the Keeweenaw peninsula, the straits of Mackinac, and the Lake Michigan sand dunes, some human-made features—such as the locks at Sault Ste. Marie and the city of Detroit, and some activities—such as farming and dogsledding. In describing the adventures of the canoe, the author also demonstrates that Michigan is bordered by four of the Great Lakes—Superior, Michigan, Huron, and Erie. The illustrations in *Paddle-to-the-Sea* include pictures of some of the named features and maps that show the locations where the canoe has its adventures as well as the wider picture of regional geography.

SkyLight Training and Publishing, Inc.

As each group researches the particulars of the target state, they may decide to contact or write to the State Department of Tourism to ask for information. Getting printed material from a state can take four to six weeks, so groups may decide instead to search the Internet for information about the state. A group focusing on Michigan could find information by going to http://www.travel-michigan.state.mi.us/region.html. Other states also have Web sites. Oregon has regional sites—for example, southern Oregon information can be found at http://so-oregon.com/. A group targeting Texas could find information at http://www.texas.usa.com/tourinfo.html. Groups may find Web sites that give information about specific states using a search engine such as AltaVista, WebCrawler, or Yahoo and by asking for the state by its name.

Students may also seek out classmates, friends, parents, or neighbors who have traveled to the target state, *interviewing* those persons to find out what they liked about the state—scenery, food, cities, recreational activities, and the like. Someone who has vacationed in Michigan's Porcupine Mountains, for example, may say that they really enjoyed the immense trees in the old growth forest, fishing for trout, the waterfalls on the Presque Isle River, and doing an interpretive guided hike with a ranger to the site of an old copper mining town, the Nonesuch.

Interview Questions

Students who find someone to interview may want to write a list of questions ahead of time—to focus the interview. The list could look something like this:

- Where did you visit in the state?
- What did you think was the most scenic spot you saw?
- What outdoor activities did you try? What did you like doing the best?
- What was the best food that you ate while you were there?
- Where would you like to go back to?

As students do the interviewing, they can record the interviewee's answers right on the list of questions and then share the information with the other members of their groups.

If the school or city library is part of a network that offers interstate, statewide check-out privileges, groups may use that library service to locate and borrow videotapes to *view* about the target state. The librarian can help them with the search and walk them through the check-out procedure. An example of a video resource that students studying Michigan may

be able to view is *Michigan Magic,* produced by Michigan Magic, 1004 10th Avenue South, Escanaba, MI 49829. If Oregon is the targeted state, students may want to order the tape of *The Oregon Coast,* produced by EMA Video, 3210 SW Dosch Road, Portland, OR 97201. A scenic drive down the coast of Oregon is featured on this video. Of course, at the library students may also find books about their targeted states that feature photographs—books such as *A Most Superior Land* (Frimodig 1983) or *Iowa: A Celebration of Land, People and Purpose* (Johnson 1995).

One member of a group may volunteer to survey local travel agencies by telephone to find out what information is available about the target state. The teacher may want to help students write a script to use while speaking with the travel agent, explaining why the students want the information. If the travel agent agrees to give the students some brochures or other printed information about the targeted state, students may then make an appointment to see the travel agent to pick up the information. A travel agent can also give students addresses for the departments of tourism for target states. For instance, if Michigan is the target state, many travel agents will have information about Michigan's Greenfield Village, Sleeping Bear Dunes, and Pictured Rocks National Lakeshores, Mackinac Island and the straits of Mackinac area, Ski Brule winter sports area, as well as Porcupine Mountains Wilderness State Park.

The first-story intellect project phase is the time when groups develop long lists of ideas and facts about target states, make copies of state maps, identify the states that border a target state (Michigan, for example, is bordered by Ohio, Indiana, and Wisconsin and by Lakes Erie, Huron, Michigan and Superior), and collect or copy pictures that they can use to design the illustrations for the final products—the top ten lists.

✳ SECOND-STORY INTELLECT

Focusing on the Goal: "The Top Ten Reasons Why We Love This State"

As a group begins the second-story intellect phase of this project, they will begin to focus on the final product—the list of the top ten facts or features of the state that they like the best. (Refer to Project Learning Log 2 at the end of the chapter.) Students will *analyze* the information that they have collected, sorting facts and ideas into "really like" and "neutral or dislike" piles. If the "really like" category contains more than ten items, they will go through the process again, honing and refining the list until they have the ten ideas and facts that they believe really are their favorite pieces of information about the target state.

To continue the scenario on the state of Michigan, the list might look like this:

- Michigan is bordered by three states and four of the Great Lakes.
- It produces cherries, peaches, apples, and tulips.
- It is home to the Detroit Tigers, Lions, Pistons, and Red Wings.
- It is home to stands of old-growth forests, such as Porcupine Mountains' hemlock-maple forest and Estivant Pines' white pines forest.
- Its natural resources include copper, iron, and timber.
- It shares the busiest locks in the world, the locks at Sault Ste. Marie, with its twin city in the province of Ontario in Canada.
- Summer recreation includes boating, fishing, swimming, and mountain biking.
- Winter recreation includes skating, skiing, snowshoeing, and dogsledding.
- The candy shops on Mackinac Island make world-famous fudge.
- The *Edmund Fitzgerald* shipwreck museum is located at Whitefish Point.

Note that the items in this list are not yet arranged in numerical/ "top ten" order. The group has finished analyzing the large amount of collected information and reached consensus on its ten favorite facts/features about the target state.

Illustrating

The next job that the group faces is to *sketch* an illustration for each item on the top ten list. The guidelines for the assignment stated that the list would describe the ideas in words and illustrate them using pictures. Students can sort through the pictures and maps that they have collected, seeking ideas for the sketches. The teacher can encourage students to use these pictures and maps as models. She can remind groups that their job is to do sketches to illustrate the top ten list—not to provide exact copies of pictures or maps that they have found. A sketch illustrating the old-growth forest could show one or two very large trees. A sketch showing winter recreation could show skis and ski poles or skates and snowshoes. The job of the groups is to provide visual cues, not panoramas.

Each group will *invent* and *draw* a logo that represents its state. The logo will be featured as part of the top ten list. A group may decide to feature

two of its favorite facts about the state when designing the logo. A group focusing on Michigan may, for example, decide that its two favorite facts about the state are that Michigan produces tulips and has lots of snow. The group may then design a logo that shows a snowman holding a tulip. Another group may decide that its two favorite facts about Michigan are that the state produces sweet cherries and it has a large number of ski resorts. That group's logo may show a cherry pie doing downhill skiing. The teacher can encourage groups to be creative and funny, in general, as they invent and draw their various state logos.

Creating a Bar Graph

Each group will use population information that they have gathered to do a bar graph that compares the total population of the state with the combined populations of the top five cities to get a feel for how "urban" or "rural" the state may be. This information is available in almanacs and road atlases. For example, the *1997 Rand McNally Road Atlas for the United States, Canada and Mexico* gives the following information for Michigan: the total population is 9,328,784 and the city populations are Detroit, 1,016,400; Grand Rapids, 193,700; Flint, 140,100; Lansing, 126,100; and Ann Arbor, 111,300. The teacher may want to help groups set up the graphs. She may want to suggest that groups space the names of the state and the five cities evenly on the horizontal or x-axis and use the vertical or y-axis for the populations. The teacher may want to help students decide on a scale for the y-axis.

Students can then use the population information to *calculate* (with a calculator) the percentage of the total population that lives in the five largest cities. For the Michigan example, the total population of the five largest cities is 1,587,600. This represents seventeen percent of the population of the state. Based on this percentage, the Michigan group may decide that most of people in the state live in smaller towns or on farms. The teacher may then ask if they need more information—such as the combined populations of all of the suburbs that are part of the greater metropolitan areas.

When a group has constructed its bar graph and completed the population study, it will mark the location of the five largest cities on the map of the state so that they can point the cities out to their classmates when they present the top ten list to the class. They may search for meaning or an explanation for the relative locations of these cities. Sometimes the relative locations of population centers in a state can tell an observer much information about the relative availability of water. Sometimes the pattern indicates the main routes traveled by early explorers or settlers or the distribution of natural resources like ores. At other times, the pattern of settlement in a state may indicate differences in climate. Larger cities tend to be located in parts of states that have more temperate climates. The group may do some more first-story work to collect new information to answer these questions.

Ordering the Items for the "Top Ten List"

When much of the other second-story work is done, groups will *generate* the order of items for the top ten lists. They work from number ten down to number one. As the group ranks the honed and refined list for Michigan, the items might be placed in this order:

10. Michigan contains old-growth forests, such as the maple-hemlock forest in the Porcupine Mountains and the white pines in Estivant Pines.

9. It is bordered by three states, Ohio, Indiana, and Wisconsin, and four of the Great Lakes—Erie, Michigan, Huron, and Superior.

8. Its natural resources include copper, iron, and timber.

7. It shares the busiest shipping locks in the world with Sault Ste. Marie, Ontario.

6. Winter recreation includes skiing, skating, dogsledding, and snow-shoeing.

5. It is home to the following sports teams: Detroit Red Wings, Tigers, Lions, and Pistons.

4. Michigan farms grow cherries, peaches, apples, and tulips.

3. The *Edmund Fitzgerald* shipwreck museum is located at Whitefish Point.

2. Summer recreation includes swimming, boating, fishing, and mountain biking.

1. The candy shops on Mackinac Island make world-famous fudge.

The groups need discussion time as they do the ranking of the items in their top ten list for their respective states. Group members need to listen to each other, find ways to compromise, and make sure that the group has reached consensus before deciding on the final rankings for the items in the list.

Developing Prototypes

Completing the rankings puts the group in position to *develop a prototype* for the final top ten list product. Each group is encouraged to make at least two possible layouts or prototypes for its list. A group may decide, for example, to develop a list in two columns, "looks like" and "sounds like," with the sketches in the left hand column and the words in the right hand column. Another arrangement may reverse the columns and have "sounds like/looks like" as the final arrangement. In a third arrangement, each written item is followed by its illustration so that the illustrations break up the

writing. The items may be arranged in one long column of ten or in two smaller columns of five items each. A group may decide on a nonlinear arrangement of items. They may want to arrange items along an "s" curve or in a spiral. The teacher may want to encourage students to be creative as they plan their layouts and to make sketches of the possibilities.

✳ THIRD-STORY INTELLECT

Testing, Showcasing, and Evaluating

When the group has completed at least two prototypes, it moves into the third-story intellect activities for the project. (Refer to Project Learning Log 3 at the end of the chapter.) The group will *try* the prototypes by showing them to the teacher and three groups of classmates and by asking which one of the prototypes the teacher and other groups likes the best. Armed with this feedback, the group will produce a rough draft of the prototype that was most popular and *test* the rough draft by showing it to the teacher and groups of classmates and by asking for feedback. The group will ask the teacher and the other groups questions: What do you like about our rough draft? What do you see as its best features? Do you understand each of the items that we have written? Have we used precise vocabulary or do we need to rewrite to clarify the ideas? What specific rewrite ideas can you give us? Do the sketches clearly illustrate the ideas in the list? What sketches do you find unclear or confusing? What specific suggestions do you have for improvement? Group members will write down the answers to these questions.

A group will also do a final check of its top ten list items for accuracy of information, correct any inaccuracies that it discovers, and add any information that members of the group agree would improve the clarity of the list. The group will *evaluate* the feedback and use self evaluation to decide what is strong about the top ten list and what needs to be strengthened.

Revising and Assessing

After evaluating the feedback, the group will *revise* the rough draft to make the needed improvements. Members of the group may want to use the dictionary to correct spelling errors or look up meanings of words. They may play with vocabulary and sentence structure to clarify meaning. They may draw sketches more carefully or use colors differently to improve the art work. As they revise, they will cross check their work with the feedback to be sure that they are making the corrections and changes that need to be made. When the group has made all of the suggested improvements, it will *repeat the cycle.* The group will take the top ten list back to the teacher and three groups of classmates and will ask for more feedback. If the teacher and classmates suggest additional clarification, the group will do another rough draft revision. When the feedback and group evaluation indicate that

the top ten list is high quality, the group will do a final, polished presentation copy of the top ten list complete with poster quality text and colored illustrations. Because the top ten lists for the whole class are to be used to create a geographic display of the United States, the final presentation copies of the top ten lists should be done on large sheets of newsprint or posterboard.

Showcasing the Project

When the day comes for groups to *showcase* their top ten lists, each group will present its top ten list to the class. All members of the group will take an active part in the presentation. The display copies of all of the lists can be done on newsprint or posterboard, but groups may choose different formats to use for the actual presentation. A group may decide to use the display copy of the list as the focus of its presentation. The group can hang the list on the chalkboard or wall, covering everything but the title with a second sheet of newsprint. For the actual presentation, the group can uncover the list items one by one—as David Letterman does on his TV program.

For instance, consider the following scenario for showcasing a project on Michigan: A member of the group begins by announcing, "This is a list of the top ten reasons we love the state of Michigan." As she reads the title, her teammates hold the second sheet of paper so that it hides the rest of the list. When she is finished reading, she takes the place of one of her teammates. The two holders move the second sheet of paper so that number ten is uncovered. As she points to the list, the new reader says, "Number ten. It contains old-growth forests like the maple-hemlock forest in the Porcupine Mountains and the white pines in Estivant Pines." He points to the illustrations and says, "And here are pictures of the maple, hemlock, and white pine trees." The reader then takes the place of the member of the group who has not yet read anything from the list. The holders move the sheet of paper to uncover number nine. The new reader says, "Number nine. It is bordered by three states, Ohio, Indiana, and Wisconsin, and four of the Great Lakes—Erie, Michigan, Huron, and Superior." She points to a map that the group sketched to show the states and lakes that surround Michigan, identifying each of the states and lakes by name. The original reader returns to that job. The reader and holders continue in this fashion until the last reader says, "And the number one reason why we love the state of Michigan is: The candy shops on Mackinac Island make world-famous fudge." She points to the picture and says, "And here is a big gooey chunk of fudge." With this last reason, the group celebrates with a cheer and the audience joins in.

As an alternative to the above presentation, a group may decide to make the display copy of the list on a single sheet of newsprint and a presentation copy with each item on its own strip of paper. If a group chooses this format, members may write each item in small lettering on the back of each strip. A member of the group will hold up the title strip and read the title. The next member of the group will hold up the number ten strip and read the information that is written on the back of the strip. Members take turns

reading the top ten list items until they are finished and, again, lead the class in cheers or applause. A group may decide to "rap" the list. Another group may decide to do a home video and show it to the class. Several days before the final presentations the teacher will want to check with all of the groups to discuss presentation formats and any special equipment that the groups might need. Thorough preparation can help facilitate a stress-free and fun presentation day. After the presentations, the top ten lists can be displayed in the classroom or in the hallways. Some schools have common areas or "showcase" areas available for such displays.

At the conclusion of the project, each group will give the teacher a *portfolio* that demonstrates the steps that it took to complete the project. This portfolio will contain evidence of gathering activities, such as reading lists, Website addresses, print-outs of downloaded information, interview sheets, or travel agency brochures. Evidence of processing activities could include sketches of the logo, the population, and top ten list prototypes. Evidence of applying may include feedback notes, revisions, and the presentation plan.

Self-Evaluation and Group Evaluation

Before members of groups move on to new groups and new projects, they will *self-evaluate* their behaviors as they work on the project. The evaluation will be done as individuals and as groups. In addition to using the rubric for self-evaluation, each student will write an assessment in his or her journal.

Students may reflect on the following:

- Decide what you did well as you worked on this project. Reflect on what you did to collect and use information and complete the product. What do you want to change next time?
- Identify two items that you want to remember about the state and one action you will use to help your group that you will use again. Tell your reasons for choosing the ideas and action.

After each individual has answered the questions privately, members of the group will share their answers with each other. The group will also answer questions such as the following: What actions did we take as a group that worked well? How did we encourage each other when the going got tough? Do we need help to do better next time? Who could help us?

Each group will *celebrate* successful completion of the project by singing a song or doing an energizing cheer together. Students may then shake hands and thank each other for helping to make a quality product. Individuals who learn to give themselves credit for doing well and to celebrate success as a team are more likely to repeat that success the next time they are asked to do a project.

SkyLight Training and Publishing, Inc.

Project Evaluation Rubric
Chapter 1: What a Wonderful State!

Performance / Criteria	0	1	2	3
Accuracy of the top ten facts/features listed about the state	Fewer than seven of the ten are complete and correct	Only seven of the ten are complete and correct	Only eight of the ten are complete and correct	Nine or all ten are complete and correct
Clarity of wording of the facts/features	Fewer than seven of the ten are clearly worded	Only seven of the ten are clearly worded	Only eight of the ten are clearly worded	Nine or all ten are clearly worded
Illustration of facts/ features in the top ten list	Fewer than seven of the ten have colorful, accurate illustrations	Only seven of the ten have colorful, accurate illustrations	Only eight of the ten have colorful, accurate illustrations	Nine or all ten have colorful, accurate illustrations
Accuracy of city locations on state map	Good for one or two of the five largest cities	Good for three of the five largest cities	Good for four of the five largest cities	Good for five of the largest cities
State logo accompanying the top ten list	Not done	Identifies the shape of the state—nothing more	Identifies the state and at least one "top ten" fact or idea	Identifies the state and at least two "top ten" ideas

Project Learning Log 1

✳ First-Story Intellect: Gathering Information

Describe what you did to gather information.

- **Read**

....

....

....

- **Visited**

....

....

....

- **Researched**

....

....

....

- **Interviewed**

....

....

....

- **Surfed the 'Net**

....

....

....

- **And . . .**

....

....

Project Learning Log 2

✳ Second-Story Intellect: Processing Information

Describe what you did to process information.

• **Sketched**

....
....
....

• **Analyzed**

....
....
....

• **Calculated/Graphed**

....
....
....

• **Developed Prototypes**

....
....
....

• **Drew**

....
....
....

• **And . . .**

....
....

Project Learning Log 3

✳ Third-Story Intellect: Applying Information

Describe what you did to apply information.

- **Tried/Tested**

....
....
....

- **Evaluated**

....
....
....

- **Revised**

....
....
....

- **Repeated the Cycle**

....
....
....

- **Showcased**

....
....
....

- **And . . .**

....
....

Chapter 2
Feeding the Birds
A Science Project

Designed to help students learn about nature and how animals depend on plants and/or other animals for food, this project involves students in designing and building a bird feeder. Along with developing analytical skills and, in particular, the naturalist intelligence in the multiple intelligences classroom, students will learn about the habits of wildlife, specifically birds—wildlife "in their backyards" that they may not have noticed before.

As students begin this project, which is an *open-ended project,* they will learn about building bird feeders and observing the different birds that visit their feeders. At the beginning of this project, the teacher may wish to distribute the rubric on page 37 so students will know the evaluation criteria. During this project, students will be identifying the species of birds they see and logging information. Students will also learn about specific foods the different kinds of birds like to eat and where they like to eat—on the ground, on a raised feeding platform, or perched on a hanging feeder.

Students may choose the materials to use in building the bird feeder, the type of feeder to make—a hanging feeder or ground feeder, a feeder for large seeds, small seeds, liquid food, or suet. The kind of bird feeder that each student makes will determine what type of food the student will be using and the placement of the feeder. Students may tailor the feeders to the sites that they have available near their homes or near their schools. A student who has a large, tree and shrub-filled backyard may choose to make a feeder to hang in a tree; a student who lives in a third-floor apartment may be able to use a ground feeder on a window ledge (if the building has window ledges and permits residents to place things there); a student who has no suitable feeding site near home may, with permission, set up a feeder on school grounds.

Before the teacher assigns the bird-feeder project, he or she may want to research the costs of materials and establish financing to help with project costs. Some schools, for example, may allow the teacher to use a school

purchase order for such supplies as wood, screening, and birdseed. The teacher may need to submit a budget request some weeks (or months) in advance to have this source of financing available. Many schools have parents' organizations that have funds available for special projects such as this one. On the other hand, the teacher may decide to inform students in the class, at the outset, that they will be responsible for paying for all of their materials. Students will need to consider their ability to pay for materials before they decide on which bird feeder to build. The teacher may want to give each student a letter to take home that explains the purpose of this bird-feeder project and the student's financial obligation, so that parents can guide their children toward choosing affordable feeders.

The teacher may also want to ask the school to purchase a class set of field guides, books that students can use to identify the birds that they see, which are useful resources for this project as well as for other projects and courses of study. Teachers of younger students may want to order *Birds at My Feeder* (Kalman and Oates 1988) or *Birds, Nests and Eggs* (Boring and Garrow 1996). Teachers of older students may prefer *A Field Guide to the Birds of Eastern and Central North American* (Peterson 1980) or *Eastern Birds: An Audubon Handbook* (Farrand 1988) (or the western bird guides for those living in western states).

Ideally, the individual student will make his or her own bird feeder. This will allow each student the greatest amount of flexibility in establishing an observation schedule once the feeder is in place. In classroom situations where it is feasible, students will do some of the work in groups of three: a contractor who keeps the group on time and on task; an architect who invites everyone to participate and to use encouraging words; and a drafter who asks teammates to clarify their descriptions or comments and leads team celebrations. Before these groups are formed, the teacher may tell students about the famous ornithologist/artist John James Audubon and the bird-watching society named in his honor, explaining that they will be acting as mini-Audubon clubs, sharing and comparing information with their team members throughout the project.

If the teacher believes that having each student make, place, and test his or her own bird feeder is not practical, as may be the case in urban settings, the teacher may decide to handle this activity as a class project or collaboration. Having one or more feeders set up on school grounds, at a nearby park, or at a nature preserve are options. If that plan is chosen, the teacher may want to involve the students in initial planning, writing the necessary letters to the appropriate authorities asking permission to set up and visit the feeders.

SkyLight Training and Publishing, Inc.

To firm up project planning, the teacher will need to have several classroom meetings with the students so that decisions such as the following can be made:

- What type(s) of bird feeder(s) will be built?
- If students are to finance their own projects, what will each student's share of the expenses be?
- What species of birds might be attracted to the feeder(s)?

If it is determined that the bird feeder is to be placed on school grounds, individual students may make arrangements to visit the feeder and log in observations on a regular basis. The teacher may need to check with the school office about observing the feeder outside of regular school hours, to be sure that individual students have permission to be on school premises at such times.

If the feeder is to be located in a park or nature preserve, the teacher may need to arrange a field trip(s) for the whole class to visit the feeder and observe bird activity. It is important to remember, however, that having large numbers of people observing a bird feeder at the same time may actually keep birds away. Many songbirds, in particular, are keenly aware of unexpected noise and movement in their environments and avoid the sources of the noise and movement.

Regarding the typical duration of this project, note that if students build the bird feeders and do the observations as individuals, they will generally need several weeks to complete the project. On the other hand, if the bird-feeder project is handled as a whole-class project, it may take considerably less time.

Before the students begin planning their projects, the teacher may want to hook their interest by reading "July, Great Possessions" from *A Sand County Almanac and Sketches Here and There* (Leopold 1949). In this selection, Aldo Leopold describes rising before dawn to listen to the birds that live on his property in central Wisconsin, as they begin the day by reaffirming their territories. The author tells of how he identifies the birds by song, not sight. After reading this selection, the teacher and class can discuss how the author learned what birds made what song. The teacher can then prompt students to think about birds in their own communities by asking the following questions such as: Do any of you hear birds singing near your homes? Do you know what kinds of birds you are hearing? How do you think you could learn what kinds of birds live near your home? Ideally, the discussion should motivate the students to complete the bird-feeder project so they, like Aldo Leopold, will have a chance to observe birds firsthand.

✳ FIRST-STORY INTELLECT

Gathering Information

As students begin the project, they will do first-story intellect information-gathering activities. (Refer to Project Learning Log 1 at the end of the chapter.) Students can begin by *visiting* a local pet store or bird feeding specialty store and by asking the people who work there what kinds of birds live in the area, what kinds of food these birds like, and what kinds of feeders are used with these foods.

The teacher may be able to arrange for a student group to do an *interview* (personal visit or by phone) with a state or county agriculture agent, someone from a local chapter of the Audubon Society, or an employee of the local soil and water conservation district or the Department of Natural Resources. These are all people who can tell students what kinds of birds live in the area and the favorite foods of those birds. To reach the local offices of government agencies, note that in many telephone directories the phone numbers and addresses for county, state, and United States agencies are often listed under "Government Offices—County, Government Offices—State, and Government Offices—U.S." or under county or state name. For example, in the local telephone book for Ontonagon, Michigan, the white-page listings for government agencies are headed Ontonagon County and Michigan, State of.

Once students have determined what kinds of birds to look for, they can gather more information on these birds by *reading* about them in a field guide such as those mentioned previously, the Peterson *Field Guide* or the *Audubon Handbook*. Several western bird handbooks are available for those teachers and students living in western states. These field guides provide information about the appearances and calls of birds, their living and breeding ranges, and differences in summer and winter plumage.

As far as building the feeder is concerned, the teacher and students may refer to such books as *The Birdfeeder Book* (Stokes and Stokes 1987) and *Build a Better Birdhouse (or Feeder)* (Wells 1996), both of which contain information about different kinds of bird feeders and the kinds of birds that use them. These books show pictures of feeders, suggest types of feed to be used in them, and give children information about some of the different materials that can be used to make feeders. The teachers and students may want to look for other resources in their school libraries. An industrial arts/technical education (woodworking) teacher may be able to provide helpful information.

Students can begin searching at home to find different materials or items from home that could be used to make a bird feeder. Some common materials that they may find are plastic pop or milk bottles, screening, wood strips or slats, flower pot saucers, pinecones, straws, thin metal or wooden rods, bread, peanut butter, and mesh bags. The actual uses of some of these materials and objects will be discussed in the section on developing prototypes.

Students can *listen* to the bird songs that they hear near their homes and guess how many different kinds of birds they are hearing. Books on birds often describe these songs in words, and children may want to match up the description with what they hear. Some songs are very distinctive. The "chick-a-dee-dee-dee" call of the chickadee is a fairly easy song to pick out of the crowd, especially since this bird is one of the less shy kinds and can be seen while she is singing. The "tyeep-tut-tut-tut" of the robin or trilling song of the sparrow may be more difficult to recognize. The most important thing for students to realize, at this point, is that they can hear several different songs that indicate the presence of several different kinds of birds in the neighborhood.

Before students make a final decision about the kind of feeder to make, they will want to observe their neighborhoods for a week, spending ten minutes on their own a day watching trees, shrubs, electric and telephone wires, fences and railings, and puddles to see what kinds of birds visit the area. It is very helpful for each student to have a field guide to use during this observation period. If students can use the field guide to help them identify the birds that they see, they will gather more accurate information about the kinds of birds that are present and be able to make more informed decisions about what feeders to make.

As students continue the information-gathering process, they may *search* the Internet. Two Web sites that contain information about birds that students can use as they plan their projects are http://www.fontbonne.edu/davis/ lcuyer.html and http://www.gc.maricopa.edu/~2dt000/ cis133/samples/birds.html. These Web sites contain information about how to start bird watching, how to identify the birds that are seen, the kinds of feeders and foods that attract different kinds of birds, placement of these feeders, and placement and use of birdbaths. The first Web site also has colorful pictures that can add fun to the research process. Children can find other Web sites by asking a search engine such as AltaVista or Yahoo to look for "bird watching."

✳ SECOND-STORY INTELLECT

Focusing on the Goal: Designing a Bird Feeder

When enough information is gathered, children will know what kinds of birds live in their neighborhoods and what these birds like to eat. They are ready to begin the second-story intellect phase of the project. (Refer to Project Learning Log 2 at the end of the chapter.) Students will begin these processing activities by analyzing the information they have about the different kinds of birds in the neighborhood and deciding what kinds of feeders they want to make or what kind of feeders the class wants to use.

Each student will *sketch* the bird feeder that she wants to make or wants the class to use. In order to do an accurate sketch, she may want to be able to go back to *The Birdfeeder Book* or *Build a Better Birdhouse*. The student may also go back to the pet or bird-feeding store to review the commercial versions of feeders. The sketch will be accompanied by a blueprint or set of plans that the student generates showing the separate parts of the feeder and the assembled feeder. Assembly instructions will accompany the blueprint. Each child will also diagram the area near her home or school where she plans to place the feeder. She will include the locations of all buildings, nearby trees, shrubs and flowers, power lines, fences, and water in the diagram. The sketch, assembly plans, and diagram will become part of the project *portfolio* that the student will use when she does her final project presentation.

Calculating Cost

Each student also needs to *calculate* the total cost of the materials that will be used to make the bird feeder. Of course, a student may be able to bring certain items for the project from home, such as empty plastic bottles, scraps of screen, straws, or mesh bags (such as those in which potatoes or onions are sold). Any wood, small rods, screen, food, or other items that needs to be purchased must be priced and the price needs to be included in the total cost for the project. The student also must include the price of the bird food in the calculations.

To insure accurate cost calculations, the student may need to revisit the pet or bird-feeding store, a hardware store, and a lumber yard. After the student purchases materials or food for the feeder, she will keep the receipts for these materials so that she can demonstrate the accuracy of her calculations. The calculations and receipts will also be part of the project *portfolio.* When all of this work has been done, mini-Audubon groups will get together so that students can show each other their plans for the bird feeder, can discuss each other's plans, and can suggest improvements or alterations. These suggestions may lead to a student's revising her cost calculations.

If the whole class is using one or more common feeders, students will need to reach consensus on the type of feeders that will be used. After various groups have had a chance to research and determine their preferences and reasons for them, there will be a class meeting during which each mini-Audubon group will present its preference to the entire class and give its rationale for the choice. Whether this rationale exercise is individual or is done by the group, reasons should address the likelihood of attracting birds to the feeder, the numbers of different bird species that the desired feeder might attract, the ease of building the feeder, the ease of maintaining the feeder, and the finances involved in building. The teacher or a designated recorder will make notes on the chalkboard or on chart paper as the preferences are proposed and discussed, so that there is an official record. Teachers will then guide students so that consensus on the type of feeder will be reached. Bird-feeder planning and building can then proceed.

Developing Prototypes

With blueprints in hand and materials available, the students are ready to develop prototypes of their feeders. On the designated day, students will bring their bird-feeder materials to class and will make their bird feeders in class. Students will work in their mini-Audubon groups as they make their feeders so that they can help and encourage each other. Sometimes an extra set of hands can be used to help with holding parts together. As students watch each other, they may decide that they want to use a teammate's plans to make a second feeder.

As students work on their bird feeders, they may develop several prototypes, such as the following:

- A feeder in which a small piece of screening is glued or stapled to a square or rectangular wood frame that has a two-inch leg attached to each corner; to be positioned on the ground at a strategic location.

- A feeder made by gluing or stapling a piece of string or yarn (to use as a hanger) to a pine cone. The pinecone is rolled in peanut butter and birdseed and then hung from a tree limb or other structure.

- A feeder made from a plastic pop bottle with three or four small holes cut out of the bottle about two inches from the bottom; a short metal or wooden rod is pushed through the plastic below each hole. A longer metal or wooden rod is pushed through the bottle near the top. Then a piece of string or yarn is tied to both ends of this longer rod so that the feeder may be hung from the designated tree limb or other structure.

- A feeder made from a mesh bag filled with suet, which has a string or piece of yarn threaded through the holes so that the bag may be hung at the designated location.

In addition to building a feeder, a student may make a birdbath by varnishing or painting a clay flowerpot saucer and setting it on the ground near the feeder location.

Teammates will help each other and will encourage each other during the feeder-making time. Later, after students place their feeders, test them, and observe how well the feeders are used by birds, they will report their findings to their teammates. Eventually, mini-Audubon clubs will be used as presentation teams.

As students build their feeders, they will each be reporting to other teammates what kind of food will go in the feeder and what kinds of birds they

hope to attract. For instance, a ground feeder could be filled with cracked corn or mixed seed to attract doves and sparrows and could be used on an apartment ledge or balcony as well as on the ground. Mixed birdseed on the pinecone could attract finches. The hanging feeder could be filled with sunflower seed to attract finches and chickadees. Woodpeckers and chickadees would be attracted to the suet. If the ground feeder is filled with raisins, it could attract robins. Students can review information that they gathered and reinforce the learning as they describe their feeders to each other. If students are building individual bird feeders, they will take the finished prototypes home for field-testing.

Regardless of whether individuals, small groups, or an entire class constructs a bird feeder, students will research—through observation and listening—the typical song of the kinds of birds that they want to see at their feeders. Teammates may practice each other's birdsongs and perform them together. They can do a grand finale by repeating all three of the songs, one right after the other. If the whole class is using a common feeder(s), the groups whose feeders were chosen will lead the class in birdsong. This birdcalling can add fun at this point of the project.

✳ THIRD-STORY INTELLECT

Testing, Showcasing, and Evaluating

Students will move into the third-story intellect phase of the project. (Refer to Project Learning Log 3 at the end of the chapter.) They will begin their *applying* activities by trying out their bird feeders. They will fill the feeders with bird food, will put the feeders in place, and will watch for use by birds. Students will want to remember that it may take birds a day or two to discover the feeder. Birds may visit the feeder during school hours, so students may want to set the feeders in place on a Wednesday or Thursday and then watch for use during the following weekend. Visits to a class feeder located on school grounds will need to be scheduled by the teacher. A parent/chaperone or classroom aide could accompany the groups to feeders on the school grounds.

If there is no adult aide available or if the feeder is off school grounds, the teacher may need to take the whole class on a field trip, as mentioned before. He or she may want to remind the students that group observations made on such expeditions will be more successful if everyone is very quiet. In addition, the teacher and the students may want to do some research ahead of time, determining what times of day to expect to see larger numbers of birds using the feeders. Peak feeding times for many kinds of songbirds are an hour or two after sunrise and mid-afternoon.

A student can *test* for effective placement by putting the feeder in different locations to see where it gets the most use by the birds. Apartment dwellers may have more than one window ledge that they can use. Students who live in single-family homes can test different locations in the yard. Spots that

are close to some kind of cover such as shrubs or evergreen trees are often preferred by smaller birds who can use the cover to hide from predators. Students can test different kinds of food to see what the birds prefer. Many songbirds, for example, prefer black, oiled sunflower seed to striped seed and students will find more birds at the feeder if they fill it with black seed. Classroom feeders can be moved to different locations on school grounds or in a park. Of course, students will need to get permission from the proper authority to move these feeders.

Observing and Keeping a Log

As students try the feeder and test different locations and foods, they will keep a log of their observations of bird activity. This log will be included in the project portfolio. Students will *evaluate* the information and decide, based on observed bird activity, which location and feed is the best for attracting birds, and what improvements would help birds use the feeder more easily. Groups will meet so that teammates can report results to each other. Teammates will discuss each individual's evaluation and help each other troubleshoot and improve the feeders, if so decided.

Revising and Assessing

Each student will then improve his or her design by rebuilding or revising the bird feeder. For example, she will refine her feeder plans and remodel her feeder or build a second model that incorporates her improvements. Then she will try out the rebuilt feeder, test placement and type of feed, if she believes that more testing is necessary, and evaluate the new information. She may choose to photograph birds using the feeder or make a videotape of bird activity at the feeder to include in her project portfolio. A class may decide to try a different kind of feeder if they can arrange more visitations to their feeders. In any case, students will want to observe their feeders at least twice during the project.

Showcasing the Project

The mini-Audubon groups will meet one last time for purposes of showcasing or making the final presentations of the bird feeders. Two small groups will combine to form one presentation group. Each student will come to the presentation with his or her portfolio, which will include the feeder sketch, assembly blueprint and instructions, diagrams showing placement of the feeder at home, cost calculations and receipts (if materials were purchased individually), feeder observation logs, photos, videotapes, and any other materials that will help describe how the student planned, built, and tested the bird feeder.

Each student will use those materials to tell the group how he or she did the project. Each student will also bring his or her bird feeder to class to show to the presentation group. In addition, students may *perform* or mimic,

for the presentation group, one song that they heard from the birds that used their feeders. Members of the group will show that they are listening to the presentation by asking clarifying questions, affirming statements made by the speaker, and paraphrasing the speaker. As closure for the project, members of the group will *celebrate* completion of each presentation by doing an energizing cheer with the presenter.

Self-Evaluation and Group Evaluation

Each individual will then *self-evaluate* his or her behaviors during the project. In addition to using the rubric to evaluate their performances, students may use their journals to record their self-assessments, using the following list as a guide for their reflections.

- Decide which thoughts and actions worked well for you during the information gathering, planning, and feeder-building processes.
- Identify at least one part of the information-gathering process that you think you did well.
- Identify at least one part of the planning process that you think you did well and one step that you want to improve the next time you do a project.
- Identify at least two things that you learned about the birds in your neighborhood that surprised you.
- Decide how much you enjoy attracting birds to a feeder and predict how likely you are to continue feeding the birds.

The mini-Audubon groups will meet one last time to evaluate their performance as a group, using the following list of questions as a guide:

- Did we disagree with ideas, rather than people, during our discussions? How did we tell the difference?
- What did we say and do to help our teammates know that we valued their ideas? Why is this important?
- What did we most enjoy about watching the birds at the feeders? Why did we enjoy that?

For the group-evaluation phase, the second question is of great importance. Students need to learn how to give themselves credit for doing well in order to be less defensive about looking for improvement. Teachers can help by remembering to ask why this is important. To conclude the project, mini-Audubon groups will *celebrate* successful completion of the project by doing their birdsongs and ending with a cheer.

SkyLight Training and Publishing, Inc.

Project Evaluation Rubric
Chapter 2: Feeding the Birds

Performance / Criteria	0	1	2	3
Sketch of bird feeder	No features are well drawn	One or two features well drawn	Three features well drawn	Entire feeder well drawn
Blueprint of bird feeder	Four or more parts missing from blueprint	Three parts missing from blueprint	Two parts missing from blueprint	No parts or one part missing from blueprint
Assembly plans for bird feeder	Feeder cannot be made by using these plans alone	Plans missing three assembly steps	Plans missing one or two assembly steps	Assembly plans are complete
Accurate prediction of bird-feeder and bird-food costs	Prediction more than 20% different from actual cost	Prediction within 20% of actual cost	Prediction within 15% of actual cost	Prediction within 10% of actual cost
Observations of bird-feeder activity	No observations entered in log	Log entries generally incomplete	One complete log entry	Two complete log entries

Project Learning Log 1

✹ First-Story Intellect: Gathering Information

Describe what you did to gather information.

• **Read**

. . . .

. . . .

. . . .

• **Visited**

. . . .

. . . .

. . . .

• **Researched**

. . . .

. . . .

. . . .

• **Interviewed**

. . . .

. . . .

. . . .

• **Surfed the 'Net**

. . . .

. . . .

. . . .

• **And . . .**

. . . .

. . . .

Project Learning Log 2

✳ **Second-Story Intellect: Processing Information**

Describe what you did to process information.

• **Sketched**

....

....

....

• **Analyzed**

....

....

....

• **Calculated/Graphed**

....

....

....

• **Developed Prototypes**

....

....

....

• **Drew**

....

....

....

• **And . . .**

....

....

Project Learning Log 3

✳ **Third-Story Intellect: Applying Information**

Describe what you did to apply information.

- **Tried/Tested**

....
....
....

- **Evaluated**

....
....
....

- **Revised**

....
....
....

- **Repeated the Cycle**

....
....
....

- **Showcased**

....
....
....

- **And . . .**

....
....

SkyLight Training and Publishing, Inc.

Chapter 3

Biography of a Senior Citizen

A Language Arts Project

For this project, students will focus on becoming skillful listeners and writers. They will interview senior citizens, asking them to tell their "stories," and gather information to use in writing biographies. As they conduct interviews, students will practice listening skills, such as responding appropriately, asking clarifying questions, paraphrasing, asking for elaboration, and checking for accuracy. As students write the biographies, they will demonstrate their abilities to plan a writing project, do a rough draft, revise and edit that draft, produce a polished product, and present their writing to an audience. They will collect their rough drafts, edited drafts, and polished products in a project *portfolio*.

This is a *genre-related project*. Biography is a genre or type of literature containing critical elements for which there are commonly accepted parameters. Student-written biographies will be expected to include those critical elements and be within the boundaries defined by the parameters. At the beginning of this project, the teacher may wish to distribute the project evaluation rubric (page 51), so students will know the evaluation criteria. The teacher may ask students if they know about biographies, perhaps reading from a published biography, and then lead the class in brainstorming a list of the critical elements of this genre. The students may use such a list as a guide as they complete the project.

For instance, it may be determined that a biography of a senior citizen should include the following elements:

- Information about the senior's parents—where they were born, their educational or work background and how they met.

- Information about the infancy of the senior including birthdate and birthplace.

- Coverage of the senior's childhood and early education.
- Description of the senior's adolescence and schooling/vocational training.
- Information on marital status, children (if any), and leisure activities/hobbies.
- Information about the senior's adult working years in and/or out of the home.
- Description of the senior's retirement or late adult years.
- Reflections of the senior about aging: the advantages and disadvantages of growing old; changes in personal activities and habits; relationships with friends and family; and physiological changes.

The students will gather their information in interview sessions with the senior citizens, during which the students will have a chance to practice their listening skills and develop richer relationships with elderly members of the community. Students will also hone their writing skills in this project. They may choose to present their final product, their biographies of senior citizens, in different ways. One student may choose to produce a professional-quality printed book, using a computer to do the word processing and a laser printer to produce the pages. Another student may write a series of journal articles using an interview format (question and answer form). Another student may choose to produce a videotaped biography, writing a script and including segments of interviews.

Students will do some work with a partner who will serve as editor and brainstorming buddy. For instance, the partner will read what her buddy has written and tell what she particularly likes about the writing and what she does not find clear. She will write specific comments on the rough draft so that her buddy knows what is clear and strong and what needs clarification. The partner will help her buddy decide on the presentation format and plan the layout of the book, journal series, or videotaped program. Buddies will celebrate success together each time they meet to edit each other's work by shaking hands and by thanking each other for helping with this project.

As another part of the project, in addition to writing the biography, each student will make a puppet or miniature mannequin of the senior citizen when he or she was a child. Focusing on a special childhood event or memory that the senior relates during the interview process and that is highlighted in the biography, the student will design this puppet/mannequin as "double" or "stand-in." When the biography is presented to the class during the showcasing stage the project, the student will use this stand-in when describing the selected event from the senior's life.

✳ FIRST-STORY INTELLECT

Gathering Information

As they begin the first-story intellect phase of this project, students will gather information to use in writing the biography. (Refer to Project Learning Log 1 at the end of the chapter.) Each student will *identify* a senior citizen to interview, one who is at least seventy years old. This person could be a grandparent or great-grandparent, a neighbor, a member of the religious congregation to which the student and his or her family belong, a resident of nearby senior-citizen housing or of a local nursing home, or a member of a local senior-citizen group. Each student will contact his or her senior partner, perhaps visiting this senior to explain the project and ask if that person is willing to be involved with the biography project. If so, a time can be scheduled for the initial interview.

Students will prepare for the interview by writing the questions that they want to ask the senior citizen, such as the following:

- In what year were you born?
- Where were you born—in what town or county, state, and country?
- Who were your parents?
- What is your earliest memory?
- Did you have brothers or sisters? (How many?) Where did you fit in the birth order in your family?
- What do you remember about your early school years? What special memory do you have of being my age?
- What did you do outside of school? Who were your friends and what were your favorite games?
- What chores did you have to do at home?
- What did you do after you finished your formal schooling? How did you earn a living? Where did you live?
- Did you marry? Did you have children?
- As you look back on your life, what do you feel happiest about? Is there anything that you would want to change if you could?
- Are there any activities that you can you no longer do? How do you feel about that?
- What do you think is a positive thing about growing older?
- What do you think is a negative thing about growing older?

The student will need two copies of the interview questions, one to use as he or she conducts the interview and one to give to the senior partner several days before the interview. Ideally, the senior partners will be allowed some time to think about their answers and organize their thoughts before the interview. Students will also advise senior partners ahead of time what will be needed to help them complete the biography projects.

For instance, when the student delivers the questions to her senior partner in advance of the scheduled interview, the student will advise the senior that she will be creating a puppet/mannequin of the subject as a child. Since the student will need some information about the type of clothing the senior wore and how he or she looked as a child, in order to design costuming for the puppet/mannequin, the student may want to suggest that the senior have a childhood photo(s) ready to show during the interview. Advance notice of this nature may be necessary in case the senior has old photographs in storage and needs some time to retrieve them. A senior may then be able to find, for instance, several photos of herself in which she is dressed in different ways—wearing playwear, a winter coat, hat and boots, swimwear, Sunday-best clothes, or schoolwear. The student could then pick which type of costume she would like to create for the senior's "stand-in."

To help students frame interview questions for the senior's reflections on aging, the teacher may *read* selections from fiction or nonfiction about aging, such as *When I Am an Old Woman I Shall Wear Purple* (Martz 1991) or *Old Age Is Another Country: A Traveler's Guide* (Smith 1995). These readings may well lead into discussions about the kinds of feedback students will want to elicit from their subjects during the actual interviews.

Interviewing the Subject

With the advance preparation done, the student will go to the senior partner's place of residence and *interview* the senior. The student may need to arrange for more than one interview session. The student will use the prepared list of questions and practice listening skills during the interview, asking the senior citizen clarifying questions such as, "I don't really understand what you mean by velocipede—could you explain what that is?" or "Was that three brothers and four sisters or four brothers and three sisters?" These clarifying questions will help the student double-check facts that are being collected so that the biography she or he writes will be accurate.

During the interviews, students may respond to answers by paraphrasing the information or checking for accuracy by asking follow-up questions, such as "So you're saying _____. Is that what you meant?" Students may also ask for expanded answers by saying things such as "You had a dog? What kind of dog was it? What did you feed it? Whose job was it to take care of the dog?"

Students will make notes during the interview. Also, a student may want to *audiotape* the interview, with the senior's permission, so that he or she can review the questions and answers to prepare for writing the biography.

The student will also ask to *view* the photos of the senior when he or she was the same age as the interviewer, if the senior has such photos available. Otherwise, the student will have to ask specific questions, such as those about typical clothing and the hair style the senior wore during childhood. At this point, the students may also ask their senior partners if they remember a song from their childhood. If so, the senior partner may teach the song to the student and the song can be part of the final presentation of the project.

If childhood photos are made available during the interview, a student may want to ask for permission to borrow them to make photocopies, using them as models for designing the puppet/mannequin of the senior citizen. In any case, the student will ask questions about the senior's clothing in the photos, such as what fabric a coat was made of and what color it was. The senior citizen may remember such details, which will help the student make an accurate reproduction of the clothing for the senior's "stand-in."

To complete the information-gathering phase of this project, students may *search the Internet* to get more information about the changes in physiology and thinking that people experience as they age. One Web site with such information is http://www.info-med.co.uk/adref/geriat/. Students may also ask a search engine such as AltaVista or WebCrawler to look for *aging, geriatrics, senior citizens,* or *growing older.* Information that is available at these Web sites may help the students to better understand the differences in mental and physical functioning that exist between them and their senior partners.

A site that may be especially good for younger students is http://www. exnet.iastate.edu/Pages/families/life/Aging/quiz/fact.grow.old.page.html. This Web site features a multiple-choice quiz about growing older. A student can find out whether a choice is true or false by clicking on the letter of the choice. The answer is also explained briefly, using simple language that even young students will be able to understand.

✳ SECOND-STORY INTELLECT

Focusing on the Goal: A Biography

When interviewing is completed, students will be ready to begin *information-processing* activities that will prepare them to write their biographies. (Refer to Project Learning Log 2 at the end of the chapter.) Students will begin these second-story intellect activities by *diagramming* or outlining the biography. A mind map or a fishbone model can be used to arrange the information into sections/chapters. Next, they will organize the information into the following categories: parents' background, family size, birthplace, and date; early childhood; adolescence; young adulthood; midlife years;

senior years; and current thoughts and reflections on aging. As they organize the information, outline, and then write the biographies, the students will need to review their notes taken during the interviews or listen to the audiotapes several times.

Illustrating

The student will do several *sketches* that can be used to illustrate the cover and the first page of each chapter in the biography. A student may decide to show a scene from the life of the senior partner on the cover of the biography and use some detail from each of the life stages to illustrate the chapters. Students also may want to ask their senior partners for permission to use copies of the senior's childhood photographs, if available, to illustrate some of the chapters.

As a class, students will revisit the first-story intellect stage by looking at published biographies or autobiographies to see how those books are illustrated before doing their sketches for their projects. An example of an interesting book for such reference is *One Woman's West: Recollections of the Oregon Trail and Settling the Northwest Country by Martha Gay Masterson, 1838–1916* (Barton 1990), a collection of memoirs of a nineteenth-century woman who was born in Missouri and traveled the Oregon Trail with her family when she was a young child. Martha Gay Masterson tells how she lived the rest of her life in various parts of Oregon, Idaho, and Washington State. The cover illustration of *One Woman's West* shows a farm like several of those that Masterson lived on throughout her adult life. The chapters are illustrated with sketches or photographs of specific places that she describes. Another illustrated biography that students may refer to is *Washington: The Indispensable Man* (Flexner 1974).

If the student has decided to do the biography as a series of journal articles, these illustrations will become the sketches that introduce each article in the series. If the student is producing a videotape, the illustrations will be featured as still shots in the video.

Processing Information

To gain some perspective on how a life unfolds, the student will *calculate* the percentages—how much of the senior's life was preschool, how much was spent in school, how much was spent working full-time, and how much has been the senior partner's "retirement." If the senior was a full-time housewife and mother, the student will use the years that she spend raising her children as her years of full-time work. The student will make a bar graph for use in the biography showing the life stage—preschool, school, working life, and retirement—on the horizontal or x-axis and percentages on the vertical or y-axis.

Developing Prototypes

Students will use their outlines to *generate* rough drafts or prototypes of their biographies. For instance, a student will use the organization shown in her outline diagram and double-check the facts with her written and audiotaped notes of the interview as she writes. She will write a table of contents, a dedication, and a foreword. Once again, she may want to review a published autobiography or biography to see what the finished product might look like. Then the student will assemble the separate parts of the biography, including the illustrations, into a mock-up of the finished book, series of articles, or videotape script.

At this point, each student will *select* an event that occurred in the early years of his or her respective senior partner. Eventually, students will be drafting scripts for final presentations about the specific events in their partners' lives, which will be presented to the class at the conclusion of the project.

To complete the second-story work, each student will *develop a prototype* of the puppet or mannequin (miniature) of the senior partner at the student's age. Creating a basic body form, the student will costume the puppet/mannequin and create the hair, using information gleaned from the interview process and from the photos that the senior partner had available. The clothing, hair, and accessories, which can be made out of a variety of materials—at the student's discretion, should be sturdy enough so that the puppet/mannequin can be handled during the final presentation or "showcasing" part of the project. If a student decides to authenticate the costuming for the puppet/mannequin, he or she may find old clothing, shoes, and hats (which may be cut apart), buttons, or other accessories at a local thrift shop.

A student who is not knowledgeable about crafting clothing for his or her puppet/mannequin may be able to get some help either from friends and relatives at home. The school's clothing and tailoring/life sciences teacher may also be consulted. Of course, a student will want to make an appointment with that teacher beforehand, explaining the project and the help that he or she needs.

✳ THIRD-STORY INTELLECT

Testing, Showcasing, and Evaluating

Students will move into the third-story intellect activities by *trying out* the prototypes of their biographies, getting together with their editing buddies to swap rough drafts. (See Project Learning Log 3 at the end of the chapter.) The buddies will read each other's rough drafts and write comments on the drafts about what they really like as well as what they find unclear or confusing. Each student will retrieve his or her own rough draft, read the comments, and thank his or her buddy for the feedback.

Revising and Assessing

The students will then *rewrite* their biographies and take them back to their buddies for more feedback. When the buddies agree that the writing is clear, students will take these second drafts to their respective senior partners, asking the senior to approve the draft. The senior partners may write comments on the draft, telling the students what they really like about the work, what they find unclear, and what corrections need to be made. The seniors will probably want to double-check the facts.

For the next step, the students should revise their biographies, as necessary, and allow the senior partner another review opportunity. This cycle will continue until the senior and the student agree that the writing is clear and accurate. At this time each student should also *test* the prototype for the puppet/mannequin, as well as the illustrations for the biographies, by showing these things to the senior partner asking for feedback. For instance, a student can ask the senior to add finishing touches to the illustrations, make corrections, or suggest different illustrations. She can also ask the senior what she or he likes about the puppet and what improvements could be made in the costume. The senior may want to help the student refine the costuming or restyle the hair of the puppet/mannequin, as the case may be.

When the senior partner and the student agree on the design of the puppet/mannequin and the final form and accuracy of the biography, they will plan the presentation or the showcasing step of the project together. The presentation will also include the childhood event selected from the senior's biography, an account of which the student will read to the class from the senior's biography or the collection of journal articles. If the biography project is a videotape, the student will plan on showing the senior's account of the event, as videotaped during the interview, making sure equipment is available in the classroom.

For the presentation, the student will use the puppet/mannequin as the senior partner's double and introduce him or her to the rest of the class. The introduction will include the senior partner's name, age, current residence, local church, club or family affiliations, and two or three other pieces of information that the senior partner really wants the class to know. The student and the senior partner will plan and script this introduction together.

At this point the student will produce a final, polished copy of the biography. Teacher and students will agree on how the students will produce the final hard copy. Younger students may decide that they want the option of handwriting or printing a final version of the book, collection of journal articles, or videotape script. Older students will probably want to use a computer to generate the final product, using a laser printer if one is available. Students who are doing a videotape will produce it at this time. In any case, the end-product will include the puppet/mannequin (the senior partner's "double") and the biography itself—whether it be a book or a collection of articles, complete with illustrations, or a videotape.

SkyLight Training and Publishing, Inc.

Showcasing the Project

Students will practice their presentations by reading their selected scenes from their biographies with their editing buddies or by showing a segment from their videotapes to their buddies. Students may also want to practice by working with their senior partners, reading from their books or journals or showing their videotapes to their senior partners. During the showcasing step of the project, students will compile their project *portfolios* which include writing and illustration drafts, pictures of the puppet/mannequin, and the final version of the biography itself—the book, the journal articles, or the videotape script.

Finally, each student will showcase his or her work. For example, a student will present the scene from the senior's life to the class, read the "current thoughts and reflections" section of the biography, and *sing* her partner's childhood song to the class. The student will then make one last official visit to her senior partner's residence to present the partner with an autographed copy of the biography or copy of the videotape, thanking the partner for all of his or her help. She and her senior partner may *celebrate* success together by singing "their" song and doing a cheer.

Self-Evaluation and Group Evaluation

In addition to using the rubric, each student will *self-evaluate* by answering questions in their journals:

- How did your listening skills improve as you worked on this project? Identify one listening behavior that you believe you do well, then identify one listening behavior that you want to improve. Suggest the actions that you can use to improve it.

- What did you learn about producing a major piece of writing? Briefly summarize what it means to plan, do a rough draft, revise, and produce a final draft. Tell what you learned about editing someone else's writing.

- What is one surprising thing that you learned about aging?

- What do you think will be the most fun about growing older?

For group evaluation, editing buddies evaluate by answering open-ended questions such as the following:

- We felt most comfortable giving feedback when we <u>(said or did what? Refer to specific collegial skills)</u>.

- We felt most comfortable getting feedback when we <u>(heard, read, or did what? Refer to specific collegial skills.)</u>.

- Our best work as partners was (_____).
- We think our partnership was like <u>(a food combination)</u> because both <u>(identify three ways in which the partnership and the food combination are alike)</u>.

After completing this evaluation, buddies will do an energizing cheer together. To conclude this project, the entire class may *celebrate* success by singing the following lyrics to the tune of "Happy Birthday," as a dedication to their senior partners: "Happy lifetimes to you! We will grow older, too. You have helped us by telling us all about you." When students have finished the song, they will do an energizing cheer.

Project Evaluation Rubric
Chapter 3: Biography of a Senior Citizen

Performance / Criteria	0	1	2	3
Publication quality of biography (final presentation copy)	More than six inaccuracies; confusingly worded sections; misspellings or smudges	Four or five quality problems	Two or three quality problems	No quality problems or one problem only
Illustrations of senior citizen's life	Few illustrations; no color; illustrations do not accurately represent senior's life story	Few illustrations; some color; weak connections to senior's life story	Few illustrations; good use of color; some connections to senior's life story	Ample illustrations; good use of color; strong connections to senior's life story
Puppet/mannequin of "school-days" senior citizen	Vague resemblance to senior during childhood; clothing looks modern	Some resemblance to senior during childhood; clothing looks modern	Good resemblance to senior during childhood; contains a few modern elements	Distinct resemblance to senior during childhood; accurate clothing "of the period"
Presentation to the class: Introduction, school-days story, and thoughts on aging	All three parts need more detail or contain incorrect information	Two or the three parts need more detail or contain incorrect information	One of the three parts needs more detail or contains incorrect information	All three parts complete and accurately presented
Song from senior citizen's school days	Not done or not understandable; difficult to hear	Half of the lyrics clearly sung or recited; more volume needed	A few words hard to understand; volume generally acceptable	Lyrics clearly sung and easily heard

Project Learning Log 1

✳ **First-Story Intellect: Gathering Information**

Describe what you did to gather information.

- **Read**

....
....
....

- **Visited**

....
....
....

- **Researched**

....
....
....

- **Interviewed**

....
....
....

- **Surfed the 'Net**

....
....
....

- **And . . .**

....
....

SkyLight Training and Publishing, Inc.

Project Learning Log 2
✳ **Second-Story Intellect: Processing Information**

Describe what you did to process information.

• **Sketched**

....
....
....

• **Analyzed**

....
....
....

• **Calculated/Graphed**

....
....
....

• **Developed Prototypes**

....
....
....

• **Drew**

....
....
....

• **And . . .**

....
....

Project Learning Log 3
✳ **Third-Story Intellect: Applying Information**

Describe what you did to apply information.

- **Tried/Tested**

....
....
....

- **Evaluated**

....
....
....

- **Revised**

....
....
....

- **Repeated the Cycle**

....
....
....

- **Showcased**

....
....
....

- **And . . .**

....
....

PART 2

INTERMEDIATE PROJECTS

A Scientist's Discoveries About Human Anatomy

A Health/Language Arts Project

As students complete this project, they will learn about the basic structure and functions of human body systems and organs by focusing on some giants in medicine—researchers who discovered what specific parts of the human body do and how the functioning or malfunctioning of an organ or system contributes to the overall health or illness of an individual. Students will select for study a winner of the Nobel Prize for medicine, a scientist who received the prize for his or her work on a specific human body system or organ. Students will research the prizewinning work and produce a medical pamphlet, such as those that are found in physicians' offices, picturing the human body and focusing on the location and function of the system or organ that is the subject of the prizewinner's study. The teacher will want to visit some physicians' offices to collect several examples of these pamphlets so that students may use them as models. As part of this project, students will study the scientists' backgrounds and create birthday cards for those selected Nobel Prize winners.

This is a *topic-related project*. The teacher may want to distribute the project evaluation rubric (page 66) at the beginning of the project, so students will know the evaluation criteria. Students often begin to study the structure and function of human body systems when they are in primary grades. By middle school and high school, health curricula include an expanded study of body systems and a study of how health is influenced by the interaction of body systems. As students do this project, they will learn new information in both of these areas; they will also learn some of the history behind the current medical understanding of human physiology and anatomy. They will employ the language arts as well as the visual arts as they produce medical pamphlets and birthday cards.

Although this project can be done by individual students, it works very well for groups of three: a graphic artist who designs the pamphlet and birthday card illustrations and encourages her teammates to celebrate success;

a calligrapher who does the lettering on the birthday card and encourages everyone to participate in group work; and a production coordinator/editor who checks the pamphlet for accuracy and clear use of language and keeps the group on task and on time. The three members of the group share responsibility for research and contributing all of the necessary materials to complete the project. Each group in the class can focus on a Nobel Prize–winning scientist and his or her study of a specific human body system or organ.

The teacher may introduce the project by reading from *Winnie the Pooh* (Milne 1927), the selection entitled "In Which Eeyore Has a Birthday and Gets Two Presents." The teacher may then lead a class discussion about how a birthday celebration honors the birthday person, using this discussion as a bridge to a consideration of how a major award, such as the Nobel Prize, honors the recipient.

✳ FIRST-STORY INTELLECT

Gathering Information

The initial first-story intellect activity that students will do is *research* at the library and/or *search the Internet* for more information about the Nobel Prize laureates who won their prizes for work involving human body systems or organs. (Refer to Project Learning Log 1 at the end of the chapter.)

The address for one Web site where students can find information on Nobel Prize laureates in medicine is http://www.almaz.com/nobel/medicine. This Web site includes links to biographical information, including birthdates (or at least birth-years) for all Nobel laureates in medicine. Students who do no have Internet access may find this information in the reference section of the library in such references as the *Dictionary of International Biography,* the *McGraw-Hill Encyclopedia of World Biography,* or the *McGraw-Hill Encyclopedia of Science and Technology.*

Following are a few examples of early scientists who won the Nobel Prize for medicine, along with their areas of study. Ivan Petrovich Pavlov won the 1904 prize for his work on the physiology of digestion. In 1906, Camillo Golgi shared the prize for his work on the nervous system. Emil Theodore Kocher won the prize in 1909 for his work involving the function of the thyroid gland and treatment of this gland when it malfunctioned. Going into later decades, in 1947 Gerty Theresa Cori won the Nobel Prize for medicine for her discovery of how the body regulates blood glucose levels. More recently, Ruta Levi Montallini won the 1986 prize for her pioneering work in discovering nerve growth factors and Peter Doherty and Rolf Zinkennagel shared the 1996 Nobel Prize for medicine for their T-cell research in immunity systems.

As each student begins the information-gathering phase, he or she should *gather* the names of three Nobel Prize–winners whose work focused on the structure or functions of a specific body system or organ, noting the work for which the prizes were given, the years in which these laureates received their prizes, and the birthdates (or at least birth-years) of these Nobel laureates.

The next step in information-gathering for this project is for the teacher to assign students to groups of three—or he or she may allow students to form their groups. Then the teacher will ask each group to review the lists of scientists' names and body systems/organs that the teammates have gathered. Groups will be asked to come to a consensus on the "top three" they would like to study; then the teacher will ask each group for the name of their number-one choice. If two groups have selected the same Nobel Prize laureate as their number-one choices, the teacher may want to ask the groups to use their number-two or number-three choices. The teacher may elect to have each group work on a different body system/organ at the beginning of the project—to eliminate such conflicts. In any case, at the end of this first session, each group should know which body system/organ and which scientist will be the focus of its study.

The next step is for students to *read* about body systems and the functions of those systems in books such as *The Body Atlas* (Crocker 1994) or any good biology textbook. Each member of a group will do some independent reading about the body system that the group will be targeting.

Students will also need to *research* their Nobel Prize–winners. They may want to "surf the 'net" to see what information is available. The Internet address given previously includes links to other Web sites containing information about the prizewinners. Students may also want to use a biographical encyclopedia to find out more information about the scientists. The school librarian can help them find information in such reference books, which often are on CD-ROM. Students may also need to do additional research on the body system/organ that their selected Nobel laureates studied.

Interviewing and Viewing

The research process may include an *interview* with a doctor, nurse, pharmacist, or other member of the community who would know about the body system and its effect on overall health.

For example, if the targeted prizewinning scientist is Emil Theodore Kocher (who described the function and treatment of the thyroid gland in his study—1909), a student may want to contact a biology or physiology teacher, explain the project, and ask the teacher for an appointment to discuss the thyroid gland and its function. The student may also want to ask the teacher if she may check out a copy of a biology textbook to use as a resource.

In connection with a study of the thyroid gland, a student may read that iodine is an essential mineral for proper thyroid functioning. She may try scheduling an interview with a dietitian or even the school nurse to research

sources of iodine in the diet, or she may visit a local drug store and ask the pharmacist about supplementary sources of iodine. The student could then find those products on the shelves and record a few brand names, the dosages of iodine they contain, the percentages of active and inert ingredients found in each product, and basic directions for use.

Whatever organ or body system is the focus of the study, students will need to collect information about the appearance and location of that organ or system. Students can *view* this information in three dimensions by using a plastic model of the human body that contains removable organs and comes with a "key," telling which of the removable parts are what organs. These models are often available in school science departments or in school resource centers. If not, the teacher may be able to borrow one from another school in the district. Reference books such as *The Body Atlas* and various encyclopedias contain diagrams and sketches of the human body, which students may also use as they gather information.

Compiling a Reference List

As members of a group conduct individual research, each member will *build* a reference list including the names of books, magazines, individuals, and places where he or she found the information. Teammates can use these individual lists to compile a reference or resource list to attach to the pamphlet that they produce. For fun and a little insight into the culture that produced a foreign-born Nobel laureate, students may want to *listen* to music from the native country of that prizewinner. A music teacher or media center/reference librarian can help students find appropriate recordings.

✳ SECOND-STORY INTELLECT

Focusing on the Goal: A Medical Pamphlet and a Birthday Card for the Scientist

Students will begin to *process* the information that they have gathered. (Refer to Project Learning Log 2 at the end of the chapter.) Groups will meet to *sort* and *analyze* information collected by individual members, eventually creating a pamphlet about the specific organ or body system under study.

As the *second-story intellect* work progresses, teammates will *generate* a mind map that organizes the information about the body system/organ under investigation. A group that is studying the thyroid gland, for instance, may include such facts as the following:

- The gland is located in the neck, it lies across the windpipe, and it has two "wings" like a butterfly.

- The gland is part of the endocrine or ductless gland system and releases its hormones directly into the blood stream.

- The thyroid hormones are necessary for proper growth and regulate metabolism.

The group would determine through research that individuals who produce too little thyroid hormone (or are hypothyroid) may feel tired, have little energy, and gain weight easily. Those who produce too much (or are hyperthyroid) may be extremely peppy and energetic and may be able to eat large amounts of food without gaining weight. Lack of iodine in the diet will slow down thyroid function and may lead to an enlarged thyroid gland condition known as "goiter."

When the group has *brainstormed* the mind map and added details, the calligrapher and editor may begin writing the pamphlet while the graphic artist works up a *sketch* that shows the location, size, and shape of the organ/system. The artist for a group that has targeted a scientist who worked with a single organ from a system—like the thyroid group—will probably want to include the other glands in the system. In the case of the thyroid group, the other endocrine glands, such as the pituitary gland and the adrenal glands, would be included in the sketches.

Developing Prototypes

The group will *develop a prototype* of the medical pamphlet and of the birthday card for the Nobel Prize–winning scientist. For the pamphlet, the teacher may want to give each group a copy of at least one pamphlet that he or she picked up in a doctor's office, which may be used as a model or a starting point for design.

Each medical pamphlet for this project will include the following:
- The name of the selected Nobel Prize–winning scientist and the year in which the prize was awarded.
- The name of the organ or system involved.
- A brief explanation of the function of that organ or system.
- Physiological indications that the organ or system is performing well.
- Physiological indications that the organ or system is performing poorly.
- A sketch showing the location of the organ or system in the body.

The teacher may want to suggest some specific ways to format the pamphlet. One format, for example, might utilize a "greeting card" fold: a standardsized sheet of typing paper folded in half so that the "front" of the pamphlet measures five and one-half inches wide and eight and one-half inches long. The front of the pamphlet could include the name of the organ and system,

the name of the scientist and year he or she received the Nobel Prize for medicine, and a sketch outlining the body and showing the location of the particular organ or body system. The front of the pamphlet for Kocher, for example, might look like the following:

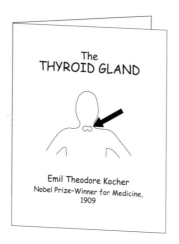

The inside of the pamphlet might describe, in words, the location of the organ or system, the function of that organ or system, and physiological indicators of good functioning. The back of the pamphlet might say: "Warning. These may be symptoms of poor functioning of (the organ or system). If you experience these symptoms, make an appointment to see your doctor." A list of these symptoms could follow the warning. Groups may develop different design formats, using the pamphlets collected from physicians' offices as models or starting points for their own designs.

Turning to the birthday card design, the dimension will be at least eighteen inches wide by twenty-four inches long, the optimum size for easy viewing when the card is on display. The card could contain a greeting or message based on the following model: "Happy Birthday, dear (scientist). We're so glad you did (the work for which the prize was awarded) because (of its contribution to our understanding of human anatomy and physiology)." For example, for the thyroid study group, the card could read: "Happy Birthday, dear Emil Theodore Kocher. We're so glad you discovered the functions of the thyroid gland and how to treat patients who had malfunctioning thyroid glands. Now we know that a healthy thyroid gland helps us feel awake and full of energy; develop skeletal structure that is well-proportioned; maintain a healthy body size; and prevent goiter."

The card might be illustrated with a likeness of the scientist (on the front) and at least one sketch—related to the work of the scientist—on the inside of the card. The teacher may want to encourage students to use humor (or even silliness) in their illustrations. For instance, the thyroid group may decide to sketch an anonymous student who is sleeping in class and label him "hypo," and then to sketch another student who is waving her arms and making silly faces and label her "hyper." The group will generate three possible illustrations and show the illustrations to two other groups to get their feedback, asking which illustration they like best and the reason for the selection. Finally, the group will design a logo for the back of the card. The logo may represent the research of the targeted scientist, the identity of the group itself, or both. For instance, for its logo the thyroid study group could draw a lobster holding seaweed in his claw, symbolizing what Kocher learned about the importance of iodine to proper thyroid functioning.

✳ THIRD-STORY INTELLECT

Testing, Showcasing, and Evaluating

The group will move into the *third-story intellect* project phase by *trying out* the prototype of the pamphlet and the birthday card. The group will *test* the pamphlet by trading rough drafts with another group for editing. Each group will read the other's pamphlet text and write comments on the rough draft telling what they really like about the work and what they find unclear or confusing. They will ask for specific clarification or expansion of the text. For instance, a note to the thyroid group might read, "We understand that someone with an overactive thyroid could be really full of energy and maybe doesn't need much sleep. What we don't understand is, do both eyes bulge out or only one? The 'bulging eye' confuses us."

The groups will review each other's pamphlet illustrations, writing comments about the parts of the illustrations that show the physiology clearly as well as comments about parts they don't understand. The thyroid group might get a note that reads, "We can see the shape of the thyroid gland, but we can't tell where exactly it is in the body from your drawing. Please revise the drawing to clarify this information."

Revising and Assessing

The group will read the feedback comments, *evaluate* them, and revise the pamphlet and the card to clarify the text and refine the illustrations, at the group's discretion. The group will also double-check all medical facts for accuracy. Then the group will show the revised materials to the group that gave them the editing feedback and ask for comments. If the editing group comments that everything seems clear, the group will begin work on the polished product for the presentation.

As part of the third-story stage, the group will decide which birthday card illustrations to use and do a mock-up or prototype of the card, one that includes a message or text and illustrations. The group will show the prototype to two other groups and the teacher, asking for feedback. The group will need to know if the placement of pictures and text makes an effective, eye-catching card, if the illustrations fit with the subject and demonstrate some humor, and if the message in the card is clearly worded.

At this point, the presentation version of the pamphlet may be typed or printed in black ink and illustrated with dark colored pencils or black felt-tipped pen, so that the pamphlet can be easily photocopied for each member of the class. Also, the group may elect to rewrite the "Happy Birthday" song lyrics to *celebrate* the accomplishments of their chosen scientist and field of study. The thyroid study group, for instance, could *sing* "The thyroid's the key—When we want energy—It needs iodine—Which is found in the sea."

As part of the revising and assessing process, the group will put together its project *portfolio.* The portfolio will include the notes from whatever interviews took place, the sketches of the organ or system that the group made during the information collecting stage of the project, the list of references that the group made while collecting information, the mind map that the group made to organize the information, the pamphlet prototype with the handwritten critique, one copy of the final pamphlet (perhaps the photocopy master), and the birthday card prototype. This portfolio will be on display in the classroom with the presentation copy of the birthday card.

Showcasing the Project

Each group will *showcase* its project, presenting the chosen Nobel Prize–winner's study of the particular organ or body system to the rest of the class. The group will first present the birthday card to the class by having two members of the group hold the card up (and open it to show the inside) while the third member reads the greeting. One of the holders will explain the illustrations to the whole class. The other holder will explain the logo or "hallmark" on the back of the card.

Continuing with the presentation, members of the group will hand out copies of the pamphlet so that everyone in the class receives one. The group will name the system or organ that the scientist studied and the function of that system or organ. The group will describe how a person feels physically when that system or organ is functioning properly. As one member of the group tells the information to the class, another member of the group will write the information on a sheet of newsprint that is taped to the front board. Group members may take turns speaking and writing. The group will end its presentation by celebrating the Nobel Prize– winner's birthday. The group will hold up the birthday card and sing their version of the "Happy Birthday" song lyrics for the rest of the class. The whole class will celebrate the success of the group by doing an energizing cheer with them.

Self-Evaluation and Group Evaluation

Each student will organize the information from the medical pamphlets by using a grid or a fishbone to record the name of that system or organ, its function in the body, physiological signs that it is working properly, physiological signs that it is malfunctioning, and the name of the scientist who won the Nobel Prize for a study of that system or organ.

In addition to using the rubric, each student will *self-evaluate* by reflecting on the following in his or her journal:

- Think about what you did to collect and use information as you did this project. What did you do well? What new actions do you want to use the next time you need to collect information?

- Identify two facts or ideas that you want to remember about your targeted body system or organ. Tell your reasons for choosing them.

- Identify at least one idea that you thought was surprising about another group's presentation and at least one fact that you already knew about that body system or organ.

- Explain one body function that you understand better as a result of working on this project.

As closure for the project, groups will display the birthday cards in the classroom. Each group will hang a blank piece of newsprint under its card. The class will use these pieces of newsprint as a graffiti wall: On two or three different days after the end of the project, the teacher will ask students to go to the wall and write down one piece of physiological evidence that signals the workings of one of the systems or organs portrayed on the cards. Recording the graffiti will help students review and remember what they learned through this project on scientific discoveries about human anatomy.

Project Evaluation Rubric
Chapter 4: A Scientist's Discoveries About Human Anatomy

Performance / Criteria	0	1	2	3
Mind map of organ/system information	Complete for one or none of the four key elements	Complete for two of the four key elements	Complete for three of the four key elements	Complete for all four key elements: organ/system, location, function, and malfunction
Pamphlet about organ/system and Nobel Prize–winning scientist	Not done or missing everything except location and name of organ/system; poor illustrations	Incomplete information about healthy and abnormal organ/system function; poor illustrations	Incomplete information about either healthy or abnormal functioning; good illlustrations	Complete information and detailed illustrations
Happy Birthday card for scientist/summary of information	Not done at all or done without illustrations, color, or humor	Summarizes pamphlet information; no color; no humor	Uses pamphlet information to honor the scientist; good use of color; no humor	Honors the scientist with affection and humor; color illustrations well done
Illustrations of organ/system functioning	Not done at all or done poorly—functioning unclear	Either normal or abnormal function illustrated—not both	Both normal and abnormal functioning pictured, but one is not clear	Both normal and abnormal functioning clearly pictured; some humor used
Logo on back of birthday card	Not done at all or a duplicate of a real greeting card company logo	Done literally; logo simply pictures organ or system	Logo shows attempt at metaphor— somewhat unclear	Logo is a clear metaphor

SkyLight Training and Publishing, Inc.

Project Learning Log 1

✳ First-Story Intellect: Gathering Information

Describe what you did to gather information.

• **Read**

....
....
....

• **Visited**

....
....
....

• **Researched**

....
....
....

• **Interviewed**

....
....
....

• **Surfed the 'Net**

....
....
....

• **And . . .**

....
....

Project Learning Log 2

✳ Second-Story Intellect: Processing Information

Describe what you did to process information.

- **Sketched**

....
....
....

- **Analyzed**

....
....
....

- **Calculated/Graphed**

....
....
....

- **Developed Prototypes**

....
....
....

- **Drew**

....
....
....

- **And . . .**

....
....

Project Learning Log 3
✳ **Third-Story Intellect: Applying Information**

Describe what you did to apply information.

- **Tried/Tested**

  ....

  ....

  ....

- **Evaluated**

  ....

  ....

  ....

- **Revised**

  ....

  ....

  ....

- **Repeated the Cycle**

  ....

  ....

  ....

- **Showcased**

  ....

  ....

  ....

- **And . . .**

  ....

  ....

Chapter 5
It's a Water-Lifterizer!
A Science Project

In early grades, students learn that people use machines and tools to do things better or more easily; later, students learn that people invent tools in order to solve specific problems. For this project, students will become familiar with the six simple machines: the wedge, the inclined plane, the wheel and axle, the pulley, the lever, and the screw. Students will then focus on this question: What series of interconnected simple machines can help us move a heavy object, such as a container of water, up an inclined surface, such as a hill? Finally, students will invent an irrigation device, which is the goal of this project.

Initially, the teacher will have students do a series of investigations or experiments about simple machines as they gather information for designing their inventions. Teams will then be formed. All of the student teams in the class will record the results from their investigations in a class results table; each team will make a copy of these results for reference. After students have investigated each of the six simple machines, they will look for tools and utensils at home that are examples of each simple machine—describing how each machine works to accomplish a household task. Students will also collect a scrapbook of information that organizes their information about these tools. Then, the teams will be presented with this problem:

> You are a team of hydrological engineers. Your community is near a river whose water can be used to irrigate the community's crops and fields, but the community is located on a hill and the river flows through a valley at the bottom of the hill. Your job, as a team, is to design and build an invention to move water from the river up the hill so that the water can be used to irrigate the community's gardens and fields.

Your machine must contain at least two of the simple machines that you have studied.

Your team assignment is to build a scale model of your irrigation invention, a "water-lifterizer" that can lift a container of 250 grams of water up a "hill" that is sixty centimeters high and empty the container so that the water effectively "irrigates" a garden that is located at the top. Your team will be expected to demonstrate this invention to the rest of the class and explain how it works.

This is a *structured project*. The teacher may want to distribute the project evaluation rubric (page 81) at the beginning of the project, so students will known the evaluation criteria. The criteria include some predetermined specifications for the water-moving invention. The students must use simple machines in the design and follow the detailed description of the task, given above, which the invention is to perform. The only way that a team can say that it has successfully completed the project is for the team to create an invention that meets the specifications. The specifications for the invention and the due date for the project are given to each team when the project is assigned. Teams will have the flexibility to choose which simple machines to use and the order in which to use them. Then they must demonstrate that their inventions will do the lifting and pouring jobs set forth in the project criteria.

This project works well with groups of three: an irrigation engineer who keeps the group on time and on task and who directs the final assembly of the irrigation machine; a project consultant who checks for agreement and understanding and correctness of assembly; and a parts supplier who gathers the materials that the team needs to build the irrigation machine and reminds teammates to use good listening skills and encouraging words.

Each team will be expected to assemble a project *portfolio*, which will eventually contain the following: a scrapbook of ads demonstrating the six simple machines; a blueprint for the "water-lifterizer"; a storyboard that shows the steps of how the invention works; a rap that the team writes about simple machines used in the invention; and photographs of the invention.

✳ FIRST-STORY INTELLECT

Gathering Information

Teams will *gather* information by *experimenting* with each of the simple machines using laboratory equipment and household tools and utensils. (Refer to Project Learning Log 1 at the end of the chapter.) The teacher will provide directions for these first-story intellect activities. Teams will be asked to *investigate* the effort that is needed to move a heavy object without using

a tool and collect data to show the benefit of using the simple machine as a tool. Teams will use each of the different classes of levers, inclined planes of different angles of incline and surface smoothness, fixed and movable pulleys, and combinations of pulleys, wheels, wedges, and screws. Teams will investigate lifting, carrying, and fastening or securing heavy loads with and without the help of the simple machines. They will *collect* data from their experiments, add their information to a table of class results, as mentioned before, and keep a copy of the class results as reference.

Students may *read* a book such as *How Do You Lift a Lion?* (Wells 1996), *Forces and Machines (Making Science Work)* (Jennings 1995), or *Exploring Uses of Energy* (Catherall 1991). These types of books will help students to gather some ideas about how simple machines can be used in inventions to do the kind of job that the students are being asked to do, the lifting and moving of a heavy object.

Students can also *search the Internet* for information about simple machines. Some addresses to try are http://www.educ.gov.bc.ca/curriculum, http://pegasus.ed.hawaii.edu/PPTwebsite/machine.html, and http://www.ed.fnal.gov/ililgrissom.html. In addition, students may try using a search engine such as AltaVista, Yahoo, or Yahooligans to find information. Asking a search engine to look for "simple machines" will result in large numbers of sites for students to explore.

As another step in the information-gathering process, students will collect ads showing examples of tools that use one or more of the six simple machines. Students may browse through magazines or newspapers—looking for ads that show different household items such as brooms, can openers, tire jacks, screwdrivers, clamps, ramps, carts, or doorstops. Each student will clip at least six of these ads and bring them to class to share with teammates.

These ads will be compiled in a team scrapbook, which will include—for each ad—a description of what kind of simple machine is represented and what task is accomplished by using that tool. For example, a broom uses a lever system that allows dirt to be swept over relatively long distances. A simple pry-type can opener is a lever. A can opener with a twist crank for opening tin cans is a combination of a lever and a screw. Clamps are levers or screws. Doorstops are, in some cases, wedges. As students analyze the various tools shown in the ads, they will determine which simple machines the tools represent, they will begin to understand the kinds of jobs that each machine can do in the water-lifting inventions.

As a class or individually at home, students will *view Bill Nye the Science Guy: Simple Machines* (Walt Disney Home Video) or the first thirty minutes of the 1968 film *Chitty Chitty Bang Bang* (MGM/UA Home Video). In the opening scene of *Chitty Chitty Bang Bang,* viewers see an invention that is really just a series of simple machines arranged to collect the food for a meal, to

cook it, and to deliver it to the table. Students may want this scene replayed several times, pausing occasionally so they may thoroughly analyze the device. Observing and recording how the invention works, students will note the tools within the device that facilitate the meal-preparing process and how they are interrelated. Some parts may be connected to each other physically; others may be connected by function.

To continue the information-gathering process, members of the team will arrange to *visit* the science department at school, local hardware stores, the hardware department of local discount stores, lumberyards, or toy and hobby shops to locate such items as small pulleys, wheels, screws, and materials for making inclined planes, levers, or wedges. The students will record where they found supplies that the team might want when it builds the working scale model of the invention. The team will compile a list of such sources for each kind of simple machine so that teammates know where to find the components for their "water-lifterizer."

✸ SECOND-STORY INTELLECT

Focusing on the Goal: Designing an Irrigation Device

Teams will begin the second-story intellect processing activities by *analyzing* the general functions performed by the simple machines. (Refer to Project Learning Log 2 at the end of the chapter.) Each team will go back to the scrapbook of ads to analyze the general uses of each kind of simple machine. A team might, for example, collect all of its ads that feature screws and clamps (which use screws to do their work) and say, "A screw can help us by holding things tightly. Objects that are joined by screws are more likely to stay together than those joined by a straight fastener, such as a nail." The team might then collect all of its ads for tools that are levers, tools such as brooms, wheelbarrows, and lawn carts, and say, "Levers help us lift objects with less effort than we would use without them. With a small effort, we can lift a large load using a lever." A team might make a similar statement for pulleys.

Brainstorming and Generating a Plan

The teacher will ask each team to analyze the process—in a real-world situation—for getting water from a river up a hill to irrigate a garden at the top, imagining which simple machine they can use to facilitate each step of the process. Students need to *generate* a hypothetical plan for their inventions, their "water-lifterizers."

For instance, a team might come up with the following plan:

> The invention will use a bucket to lift water out of the river, lift the bucket of water up the hill, tip the bucket over to spill out the water, and move the water a small horizontal dis-

tance to a garden once it gets to the top of the hill. We begin with our bucket in the river. We could have a rope that goes around a pulley. We will attach one end of the rope to the handle of the bucket that is in the river. We could have the other end of the rope attached to the handle of another bucket that is sitting next to a large rock at the top of the hill. This second bucket will be sitting on the high end of a teeter-totter (a lever) that has its fulcrum at the very edge of the hill, so that when the end of the teeter-totter on which the bucket is sitting drops down, the teeter-totter drops out from under the bucket. We will tie the other end of the teeter-totter down.

When we are ready to irrigate our garden, we will use a lever to put the large rock into the second bucket. A knife attached to the lever will cut the rope that is holding the teeter-totter. The weight of the rock will make the bucket side of the teeter-totter fall. As the teeter-totter falls, it will drop out from under the bucket and the bucket with the rock will fall down the hill. As this bucket falls, the rope over the pulley will pull up the bucket of water from the river. The top of the rising bucket will hit a bar sticking out of a wheel and spin the wheel. The wheel will spin just fast enough so that the bar will come around and hit the bottom of the bucket full of water. The bucket will tip and the water from the bucket will spill into a trough, which is just an inclined plane with sides. The water will run down the trough and into the garden.

At some point during the planning phase, the teacher will conduct a classroom meeting to discuss the actual building of scale models of the water-moving machines and how teams will test those scale models. If the class does not usually meet in a science room that is equipped with at least one sink, the teacher will arrange to meet in a room that has a sink, in order to test the machines. He or she may also want to ask the teams to bring towels or sponges to the testing session with them, so that they can mop up any water that spills. The teacher can ask teams to start brainstorming ways to get the materials that they need to make their "water-lifterizers." The teacher should make sure a camera will be available so photos can eventually be taken of the scale-model inventions.

There are several strategies students may use to gather supplies for this project. Teams might be able to use some items that individual teammates have at home. For instance, students may decide to use paper cups as buckets, string as rope, rulers as levers, and driveway gravel as rocks. A science teacher might be able to loan pulleys, fulcrums, fulcrum supports, and small carts to teams. Students also might be able to use some of the equipment that was provided for the investigation and experiment phase of the project as they build their scale models. As a team, students might agree to pool funds to buy some special items. Later, teams will be calculating exact costs

for scale models of their inventions. If money for purchases will be needed, arrangements for funding should be made ahead of time.

Regarding purchasing of materials for the project, parents of the students should be advised ahead of time if their children will be expected to contribute money on their own. Teachers may first want to find out if financial assistance for this project is available from the school itself or from the PTO/PTA, school booster club, or other interested parent group. Parent/teacher groups will often, if given advance notice, provide funding for special projects. Of course, the teacher will want to settle such financial matters before teams begin work on their projects.

At some point in this planning phase, the teacher will set a schedule for the project and inform students of the following deadlines: the date by which materials for the scale model must be assembled; the date on which the scale model will be assembled in class; and the date or dates for initial testing of the prototype irrigation device. The teacher will ask each team to provide its own "river" and "garden" water containers. Plastic milk, bleach, or laundry-detergent bottles, which have been thoroughly rinsed out and have had their narrow tops cut off, work well as water containers for this project. The teacher will ask each team to provide its own "waterproof" hill, suggesting a large flowerpot, a pail, or a large cooking pot—turned upside down—as possibilities.

Storyboarding and Illustrating

The teacher will ask the team to *storyboard* the functioning of the irrigation device. The storyboard will use a comic strip (or animated cartoon) format to illustrate the steps in the functioning of the invention. Initially, teams may use a rough storyboard format as they plan and experiment with different invention designs. The final storyboard can be done using a large strip of newsprint and colored markers. Each step in the functioning of the invention will appear in its own square on the storyboard.

For instance, to illustrate the proposed plan for the invention, the first square on the storyboard might show the teeter-totter tied in place with one bucket ready to receive the rock and the other bucket in the river. The second square could show how one end of a lever flips the rock into the bucket while a knife tied to the other end of the lever cuts the rope holding the teeter-totter in place. The storyboard would continue, action by action, until the last few squares show the water spilling into the trough and running down the trough and into the hilltop garden.

As members of the team visualize what is happening to the bucket full of river water and how the different machines interact in the invention, they may find that they have overlooked a problem that will interfere with the functioning of the invention. For example, a team might get the bucket of water to the top of the hill and then have no way to get the bucket to tip over so that the water spills out. The team might get the bucket to tip when it reaches the top of the hill only to have the water miss the trough to the

garden. If the team does the storyboard activity, showing the invention in action and describing what is happening in each picture, members of the team will be more apt to predict problems and troubleshoot before finalizing the design.

Developing Prototypes

For the next step, each team will *sketch* a "blueprint" of its invention, essentially an exact plan or schematic showing the design of the irrigation device. The team will label each part of its irrigation device to tell what that part is, what material that part is made out of, and how that part will be connected to the rest of the invention. Students will note that certain parts, those not physically connected, need to be the right size or the right distance apart so the invention will function as desired when finally assembled. Included with the blueprint will be a list of the materials that the team will need to make the invention.

Calculating Cost and Purchasing Materials

To *calculate* the total cost of building the invention, the team will start with the list of materials. The team can use the price information gathered from the store visits to do the necessary calculations. The teacher may want to help the teams review the process for computing percentages, so that applicable sales taxes can be included in the totals.

Members of each team will pool their resources, as arranged ahead of time, contributing money to buy the materials or providing the materials themselves. The supplier of each team will make purchases, as necessary. He or she may elect to assign some purchasing responsibilities to other teammates. When the supplier has gathered all the materials, the team will start to *build a prototype,* a scale model of the water-moving machine.

✳ THIRD-STORY INTELLECT

Testing, Showcasing, and Evaluating

Once the team has done the planning and has built the prototype, it is ready to begin the third-story intellect phase of the project by *testing* the invention to see if it works. (Refer to Project Learning Log 3 at the end of the chapter.)

Each team will create its "river" by filling a large container with water. The team will then assemble the scale model of its "water-lifterizer" so that the device for scooping water out of the river is positioned over the river water. The team will place another large water container at the top of its "hill" (the inverted pail, flowerpot, paint can, or other item that the team brought to use for this purpose). The team will position the top end of the scale model so that the "garden" (the container at the top of the hill) will receive the water.

Each teammate has a special function during this phase of the project. The project consultant will direct the actual assembly of the scale model; the irrigation engineer will check the assembly against the blueprints to be sure that the invention is being put together as planned. As a facilitator, the parts supplier will help all team members remember to be patient and use encouraging words as they assemble the machine. Once the invention is assembled and checked, the team will test its use. It will start the action of the invention and watch to see if the invention will fill the bucket of water and empty it so that the water goes into the garden. Each team will have a test-buddy team watching the trial run with them.

The teams will *evaluate* how well the invention worked. If the invention did its job, the team will be ready to demonstrate its invention to the whole class. If something went really wrong—for instance, if the bucket of river water stayed in the river or a rope broke or the water spilled back into the river—the team, along with its buddy-team, will brainstorm solutions to the problem. The inventing team will *rebuild* the invention to improve its performance. If the rope broke, the inventing team might decide to use a heavier rope. If the bucket stayed in the river, the inventing team could decide that it needs to reposition the teeter-totter on top of the hill or use a heavier rock. If the water does not get to the garden, the inventing team might decide to extend the trough that catches the water that spills out of the bucket.

Revising and Assessing

If there was a problem during testing, the team might find it helpful to go back to the *storyboard* to visualize what went wrong and how it can be fixed. After redesigning and rebuilding, a team will *retest* the invention, reevaluate its performance, and discuss what, if any, improvements the team still wants to make. When the testing, evaluating, and rebuilding are done, the team will have a final, presentation model of the invention ready to demonstrate for the whole class. The team will also make a polished, presentation copy of the storyboard reflecting any last-minute design revisions. Together, the team will write a *rap* that will help the group remember the names of the simple machines that were used in the building of its invention—as well as the individual jobs those machines do to complete the irrigation process.

Showcasing the Project

Each team will *showcase* its invention by demonstrating the invention to the rest of the class. Remembering their rap, teammates will be able to explain which simple machines they used, their reasons for using those machines, and how they sequenced or connected the machines to make their irrigation device. Members will use the storyboard to illustrate the explanation and they will take turns doing the explanation.

For this showcasing part of the project, the engineer will explain the first storyboard square to the class while the consultant and the supplier hold up the storyboard. The engineer and the consultant will then trade places; the consultant will explain the second square. Next, the consultant and the supplier will trade places and the supplier will explain the third square. The teammates will continue the rotation until the explanation is complete and then demonstrate their invention for the whole class, *celebrating* success by singing their rap. The class will then do an energizing cheer with the team. All of the scale models of the "water-lifterizers," along with the project portfolios, will be displayed in the classroom for several days.

Self-Evaluation and Group Evaluation

In addition to using the rubric, as a closure activity each individual will write a self-evaluation entry in his or her journal.

Students will begin the self-evaluation by answering questions such as the following:

- What is one household tool that is really a simple machine that you use a lot?
- How does this tool make your life easier?
- Can you think of a part of your body that acts as a simple machine? How does this part of your body work to accomplish a task?

Also, students will reflect on all the different intelligences they used as they did the water-lifterizer project. They may be prompted with the following points:

- You did some kinesthetic work as you help the team perform experiments.
- You did some logical work as you collected and organized prices.
- You did some visual work as you did the storyboard.
- You did some rhythmic work as you did the rap.
- You did some naturalist work as you sorted pictures (ads) into simple machine types.
- You did some verbal work as you described the sequence of motions and the invention design.
- You did some interpersonal work as a member of a team.

To do some group evaluation, ask teammates to consider how they worked together: When did each student feel the most comfortable as a learner? When did each student feel the least comfortable? What did each

student do to increase his or her comfort level in that group situation? As teammates discuss their comfort zones with each other, they will consider how their different comfort zones complemented each other—noting when there were difficult times for the team in general. Teammates will brainstorm ways to alleviate such discomfort when they find themselves involved in group work in the future.

Finally, as a team, students will complete the following metaphor: Inventing a "water-lifterizer" is like (learning a physical skill such as walking or writing or tying shoes) because both processes (include at least two similarities you as a team can determine).

Project Evaluation Rubric
Chapter 5: It's a Water-Lifterizer!

Performance / Criteria	0	1	2	3
Rhyme and rhythm in rap about simple machines	No rhyme or rhythm schemes	Some rhyming; inconsistent rhythm	Consistent rhyming; some rhythm breaks	Consistent rhyming and rhythm
Storyboard showing irrigation device (invention) in use	Three or more water-transport steps missing or unclearly described	Two water-transport steps missing or unclearly described	One water-transport step missing or unclearly described	All water-transport steps shown and clearly described
Blueprint for assembling invention	Could not be used for invention assembly without extra help (separate directions)	Invention assembled; three or more corrections on blueprint needed	Invention assembled; two corrections on blueprint needed	Invention assembled; one (or no) corrections on blueprint needed
Scrapbook of print ads	Ads show only three of the six simple machines	Ads show only four of the six simple machines	Ads show only five of the six simple machines	Ads show all six of the simple machines
Test of invention	Invention did not work at all	Invention worked with minor assistance; spills occurred	Invention worked with minor assistance; no spills	Invention worked with no assistance or spills

Project Learning Log 1

✳ **First-Story Intellect: Gathering Information**

Describe what you did to gather information.

• **Read**

....

....

....

• **Visited**

....

....

....

• **Researched**

....

....

....

• **Interviewed**

....

....

....

• **Surfed the 'Net**

....

....

....

• **And . . .**

....

....

Project Learning Log 2
✳ **Second-Story Intellect: Processing Information**

Describe what you did to process information.

- **Sketched**

....
....
....

- **Analyzed**

....
....
....

- **Calculated/Graphed**

....
....
....

- **Developed Prototypes**

....
....
....

- **Drew**

....
....
....

- **And . . .**

....
....

Project Learning Log 3

✳ **Third-Story Intellect: Applying Information**

Describe what you did to apply information.

- **Tried/Tested**

....
....
....

- **Evaluated**

....
....
....

- **Revised**

....
....
....

- **Repeated the Cycle**

....
....
....

- **Showcased**

....
....
....

- **And . . .**

....
....

Chapter 6

Creating a Field Guide for Manufactured Objects

A Visual/Language Arts Project

As students do this project, they will learn to carefully observe objects or structures built by human beings in order to identify their visual features and elements. Students will distinguish among different styles of such items and classify data in the form of field guides, the usual topic of which are natural phenomena such as flowers and trees. At the outset of the project, students will begin by selecting a category from the vast array of manufactured items around them, items such as furniture, signs, appliances, vehicles, buildings, windows, apparel, and traffic signs.

Working on this project will help students increase their perception and reflection skills. Not only will students use the scientific processes that naturalists employ to collect and organize information as they create field guides, they will also use the creative processes visual artists employ.

This is a *template project.* The teacher may want to distribute the project evaluation rubric (page 93) at the beginning of the project, so students will know the evaluation criteria. Field guides generally follow the same accepted structure. These guides are divided into sections, with each section representing a different general type of object. Each general type consists of a number of species that have similar overall shapes and other characteristics in common. The page in the field guide that introduces a general type of object will contain a summary of the visual elements that define the type. Each species within a type is then described in its own entry. A photo or sketch illustrates each species. Some field guides include a small map with a shaded portion that shows the native range of each species.

As students begin this project, they will inspect a number of already-published field guides (some specific suggestions are given in the next section of this chapter). Students will become familiar with some of the different layouts and will consider the form that their field guides will take. Like the authors of published field guides, students can show individual creativity in

their selection of illustrations and in the vocabulary that they use to describe types and species.

This is a project that is well-suited for groups of four students, all of whom will not only collaborate on the field guide but will have special duties. The teacher may assign such groups and then allow students to determine who will take on which role. Possible role definitions follow.

Team Roles

- The project manager, who keeps the group focused and on deadline and assigns specific production details to teammates.
- The materials coordinator, who collects photos, readings or original text, and other project materials and brings those materials to all group work sessions.
- The facilitator, who checks for agreement on project design and mutual understanding of content as the group works together, generally helping the group reach consensus.
- The celebration coordinator, who encourages teammates to keep going when the work gets tough and has the group take energizer breaks, leading the group in a special energizer (a cheer and/or physical exercise) to celebrate success at the end of each work session.

The teacher will also assign each group a buddy group as the project begins. Buddy groups will work together to give each other evaluation and feedback about prototype field guides. Helping each other decide on final designs for field guides, buddy group members will critique covers as well as page layouts for prototype field guides. They will read text and comment on what is clear and what is not, on which sketches are clear and which are not, and on when they believe that another group's field guide is ready for final production.

To introduce students to the concept that different visual elements, styles, and techniques produce items that can be classified into general types, the teacher may want to have students go through an exercise using fine art. For this exercise, teachers will display a few reproductions of famous paintings, choosing from different categories of artwork—paintings by Renaissance artists such as da Vinci and Michelangelo, by impressionists such as Gauguin and van Gogh, and by American realists such Wyeth and O'Keeffe, for example. Taping a small magnet to the back of each piece of art, the teacher will display each picture by itself for a few seconds, not disclosing information on the art category but simply directing the students to observe the painting closely. Then the teacher will show all the pieces together on a flat metal surface in the classroom, such as some chalkboards or large metal cabinets.

To continue this visual exercise, the teacher will then ask the class to help him or her group the pictures by general category or type, determining how many different categories or types they think are represented by the pictures they have chosen. By closely observing subject matter and placement, style, use of color and detail, background, and brush work, students will generally (with a little prompting, perhaps) be able to group the paintings by type—from the eras of the Renaissance, impressionism, and American realism, for example. After this exercise, the teacher will advise the students that they will be using the same perception skills (analyzing and reflecting skills) that they used for this visual exercise for their work on their field guide projects, identifying and classifying various manufactured structures or objects in their environment.

Each group will develop a project *portfolio* that will eventually contain the following: the field notebooks that teammates used to make their initial field notes about objects (one field notebook per group member); the prototype cover sketches and page-layout sketches used to develop the final field guide; the rough drafts of the text of the guide including written feedback from the buddy group; and the photos used as models for the species illustrations. The complete portfolio will be displayed with the final, polished field guide when the project has been completed.

✳ FIRST-STORY INTELLECT

Gathering Information

Students will begin the first-story intellect phase of this project by becoming more familiar with field guides. (Refer to Project Learning Log 1 at the end of the chapter.)

First, students will *research* the layouts of published field guides in the naturalist field by looking at such books as *Eastern Birds: An Audubon Handbook* (Farrand 1988), *A Field Guide to the Birds of Eastern and Central North America* (Peterson 1980), *A Field Guide to Wildflowers of Northeastern and Northcentral America* (Peterson and McKenny 1968), and *Trees of North America* (Brockman and Merrilees 1968). Students will *read* the text portions (the descriptions of species) in the selected field guides, to become familiar with the typical writing style used in this unique genre.

Noting categorizing systems used in the various naturalist field guides they examine, the students will consider which systems might lend themselves for use in categorizing manufactured objects. As students *view* the field guides, they will also make notes about ways in which the guides organize text, pictures, and maps. Students will determine ways in which the guides compare similar species and identify elements that are used to distinguish among species, as well as how the guides present information in the table of contents and index.

For design ideas for their field guides, students will look for helpful features such as general outlines showing the different species types that are often printed on the front or back flyleaves of naturalist field guides. Students will also note how the field guides introduce special terms. *Trees of North America,* for example, contains a short explanatory section on basic features of trees. Most field guides have a special section describing how to use the guide. Students will keep a record of the special features that they find in the field guides that they survey to be used as the groups determine the design of their field guides.

Each group will then examine a list of categories of manufactured objects and select one for which the group would like to develop a field guide. In addition to those categories mentioned at the beginning of the chapter, the teacher may also suggest other categories, such as cookware, carpenter's tools, and jewelry. A group may propose a category of its own. Each group will discuss its choice with a buddy group and with the teacher. The group will tell what the members like about the category and the reasons that the members believe a field guide for the category will be interesting for others. The teacher may steer a group toward a different category if he or she believes that the category the group has chosen might not be broad enough or might be impractical for developing a field guide. For instance, if a group in a school located in a rural area chooses military apparel as its category, the students may find it difficult to do field work and find places (such as museums) where they may view actual examples of historic military gear.

Once a group has picked its category of manufactured objects, members of the group will become careful *observers* as they do the necessary research. Each member of the group will keep a notebook in which he or she records sightings of objects of the chosen category, which that person encounters "in the field." This "field notebook" will include a verbal description of the example, a sketch of the item, the location where the group member made the sighting, the date, and the time. Each group will also find a way to photograph at least twelve different objects that are examples of the field-guide category that they spot in the field, borrowing a camera if need be or possibly buying a relatively inexpensive "disposable camera." The group will use this collection of photographs to analyze and compile information as well as to illustrate the field guide. Having such photographs available will enable group members to observe the objects more closely over a period of time, analyzing their features and making detailed comparisons among the various objects.

A productive way for individuals to get information about many different objects that belong to the field-guide category is for the individuals to *visit* a business that sells or displays these objects. Students may visit furniture or appliance stores, car dealerships, clothing stores, discount stores, and so on, depending on their chosen categories, to make field sightings. For example, if their category is signs, group members may examine storefronts, homes, street corners, and roadsides to find examples. If the category is buildings, a real estate agent may be able to help students with pictures of buildings that are for sale. In any case, some exploration of their environment, their community, will be necessary for students to complete the field work for this project.

For more information about the field-guide category, each student will *search the Internet* using the chosen category as the key word. A search engine such as AltaVista, WebCrawler, or Yahoo will give students many Web sites to investigate.

✳ SECOND-STORY INTELLECT

Focusing on the Goal: A Field Guide

Each group will begin the second-story intellect phase of the project by *analyzing* the field notes and photographs taken by group members to determine species of objects. (Refer to Project Learning Log 2 at the end of the chapter.)

Sorting and Classifying

This is where students will really use their powers of perception to *sort* the objects and *classify* them by types. A group that is working on furniture, for example, may decide to define types by function: seating, tabling (supporting food, plants, or other objects), sleeping, bookcasing (shelving), and drawer configuration (as for a dresser or chest of drawers). The group may decide to define types by visible material rather than function, in which case the furniture types may be wood, fabric, metal, plastic, and glass. A group that is working on vehicles may decide to define types according to perceived size: tiny, small, mid-sized, large, and giant. A group that is working on signs may decide to define species according to illumination: external, internal/hidden, and visible glass tube. The teacher will help groups by reminding them to look for visual cues that they will use to sort the examples into the different types that they will define. Each group will *generate* a list of general types for its field guide, define and describe the visual elements of those general types, and sort the photographs accordingly.

Each object shown in an individual photograph may then become a distinct species. Two objects will be judged to belong to the same species only if they are so identical in all particulars that group members decide that the objects would be almost impossible to tell apart from each other without extremely detailed examinations. If two different teammates both brought in a photograph of the same make and model of bookcase, for example, the group may decide that only an examination of the two pieces for small differences in surface texture or appearance would provide someone with enough information to tell them apart. These two bookcases would

then represent a single species. Members of the group will define and describe each species, again paying close attention to visual features of the objects that represent the species.

Each group will *calculate* the percentage of objects in the field guide that belong to each general type. The group will then predict whether or not it believes that these percentages would be the same if the calculations included all of the objects in the category that could be found in the community. The group will give its reasons for the predictions. A furniture group may say, for example, that it believes that the percentage of wooden furniture in its sample is higher than other furniture types because of the style of furniture store group members visited to make their sightings. Or the group may say that it believes the number of drawer pieces in a typical dresser is about right because the group members got their examples in their own homes. In making their predictions and explaining the reasons for those predictions, members of the group will need to think about where they collected their sightings and how well those places represent the overall community.

Illustrating

Each group will *draw* three different cover illustrations for its field guide. A group may want to go back to the nature field guides and look at their covers to see what elements to include. *Trees of North America,* for example, shows a hemlock twig with cones, a tulip-tree leaf with flower, a buckeye leaf, and a red-oak leaf with acorns. Four different broad classes of trees are represented by these four different species. *Wildflowers of Northeastern and Northcentral America* shows a trillium, a showy lady slipper, and a showy orchis [orchid]—three species from a single general type. The group will show its illustrations to its buddy group and ask which illustration the buddy group likes the best and why. The field-guide group and the buddy group should reach consensus on a preferred cover for the field guide before they end the discussion.

Developing Prototypes

Once the types of objects are defined, the specific objects are sorted, and each species is defined, the group will *develop a prototype* of its field guide. The group will decide the order in which to arrange the types of objects; whether to use the left-hand-right-hand-text-illustration layout or to use the chunked-text-with-collected-illustrations layout; where, how, and whether to include maps showing territories occupied by the field-guide types of objects; and what, if any, illustrations to use on the flyleaves. In addition, the group will write the "how to use this field guide" introduction; do the "basic features of these objects" piece; lay out the title page; and write the biographical information about the group members—the authors—for inclusion on the back cover. The group will also *design* a logo to accompany the name of their "publishing" group on the title page. The logo will incorporate visual features that are shared by all of the main types of objects that the group defined.

✳ THIRD-STORY INTELLECT

Testing, Showcasing, and Evaluating

Each group will move into the third-story intellect phase of the project by *testing* the prototype field guide. (Refer to Project Learning Log 3 at the end of the chapter.) The group will begin by showing the prototype to its buddy group and asking for feedback.

As one group reads the other's field guide and examines the accompanying illustrations, members will write comments to explain what they like about the field guide and what needs clarification or revision. This critique, written on a separate piece of paper, will include comments on the overall layout of the field guide—the cover, the title page, the text and illustrations, and the logo designed by the group. As the two groups *evaluate* each other's field guide prototypes and exchange critiques, some follow-up discussion may be necessary so each group will have enough feedback to agree on what needs to be improved.

Revising and Assessing

The field-guide group will *revise* the rough draft to incorporate the changes that it discussed with the buddy group. They will take the revised field guide back to the buddy group and *repeat the cycle* of getting feedback, discussing and evaluating, and making revisions. When both groups agree that the field-guide design is clear, that the cover is effective, and that the title page, introduction, and back-cover biographies are publication quality, the field-guide group will produce the polished, presentation copy of the field guide. The presentation visual will include sketches that show the visual elements.

> The group will produce a presentation visual in the form of a mind map, an outline, or a fishbone that includes the following:
>
> - The name of the general category of manufactured objects the group chose to study.
>
> - The general types that the group defined within the category.
>
> - The visual elements of each type.
>
> - At least two species that fit within each type.

Showcasing the Project

Each group will *showcase* its field guide by using its visual as a presentation aid as the group describes to the class what category of manufactured

objects it chose to work with, the group's reasons for choosing that category, the general types of objects that it defined within that category, and the visual elements of each type. The group will use one species from each type to show the class what the visual elements look like for that species. Each group will receive a round of applause or another energizing cheer from the class as a *celebration*.

Self-Evaluation and Group Evaluation

In addition to using the rubric, each individual will self-evaluate, noting reflections in their journals.

> Students will complete the following statements in their journals and share answers with each other:
> - Two important things that I learned about being a careful, discriminating observer are. . .
> - My personal definition of "a visual element" is. . .
> - Different types of a category of manufactured objects may have one common visual element, but there are different types because. . .

As a closure step to the field-guide project, each individual will select one visual element from each object type in the field guide and combine these elements to create a new visual system. A member of the furniture group may, for example, design a chair that has an attached table, a drawer built into a canopy, shelves built into the back, and a seat that unfolds into a bed. The person will do a sketch of the new piece of furniture that is the new visual system. Members of the group will then explain their new visual systems to each other, identifying which element in the system came from which broad type within their category of manufactured objects. The group members will collaborate to create a new group object.

> Members of the group will evaluate themselves as a group by answering these questions:
> - Two important things we learned about reaching agreement versus reaching consensus are. . . .
> - Two features of our field guide that we are really happy with are. . . .
> - If we were to do another field guide, one thing that we would do differently is. . . .

The teacher will choose an area in the room to display the completed field guides. Each group will share its newly created object with the rest of the class. The class will *celebrate* by telling each group they like (or even LOVE) their new creation.

Project Evaluation Rubric
Chapter 6: Creating a Field Guide for Manufactured Objects

Performance / Criteria	0	1	2	3
Completeness of field-guide cover (illustrations, logo, and biographies)	Three elements missing or unclear	Two elements missing or unclear	One element missing or unclear	All three elements present
Clarity of introductory and how-to-use sections in field guide	Five or more instances of unclear writing or instructions	Four or more instances of unclear writing or instructions	Two or three instances of unclear writing or instructions	One (or no) instances of unclear writing or instructions
Descriptions of general object types in field guide	Five or more instances of unclear writing	Four or more instances of unclear writing	Two or three instances of unclear writing	One (or no) instances of unclear writing
Descriptions and illustrations of species in field guide	Only one description/illustration; five pages need clarifying work	Only two descriptions/illustrations; three pages need clarifying work	Three descriptions/illustrations; two pages need clarifying work	More than three descriptions/illustrations; one or no pages need clarifying work
Visual presentation of field guide	One missing element; at least two items need clarifying	One missing element; at least one item needs clarifying	No missing elements; at least one item needs clarifying	No missing elements; general category, types, and species all clearly identified and illustrated

Project Learning Log 1

✳ First-Story Intellect: Gathering Information

Describe what you did to gather information.

• **Read**

....

....

....

• **Visited**

....

....

....

• **Researched**

....

....

....

• **Interviewed**

....

....

....

• **Surfed the 'Net**

....

....

....

• **And . . .**

....

....

Project Learning Log 2

✳ **Second-Story Intellect: Processing Information**

Describe what you did to process information.

- **Sketched**

  ....
  ....
  ....

- **Analyzed**

  ....
  ....
  ....

- **Calculated/Graphed**

  ....
  ....
  ....

- **Developed Prototypes**

  ....
  ....
  ....

- **Drew**

  ....
  ....
  ....

- **And . . .**

  ....
  ....

Project Learning Log 3
✴ **Third-Story Intellect: Applying Information**

Describe what you did to apply information.

- **Tried/Tested**

....
....
....

- **Evaluated**

....
....
....

- **Revised**

....
....
....

- **Repeated the Cycle**

....
....
....

- **Showcased**

....
....
....

- **And . . .**

....
....

SkyLight Training and Publishing, Inc.

PART 3

ADVANCED PROJECTS

Chapter 7

Are You What You Eat?

A Nutrition/Social Studies Project

Researchers agree that there is a strong link between diet and chronic disease. Health-literate students can explain the impact of diet on personal health. They know how diet affects the functioning of body systems and the nutritional habits that can help them maintain good health and prevent disease. As students do this project, the focus of which is a role play on nutrition, they will develop their "health literacy"—learning how ideas about diet and nutrition and the effect of diet on health have changed in the past 200 years. Students will gain knowledge of the eating habits and daily activities of Americans during the early 1800s and how their food and homeopathic remedies affected their health. Students will also acquire information about eating habits of contemporary people with busy lifestyles and the healthiness (or unhealthiness) of this way of eating.

This is an *open-ended project.* The teacher may want to distribute the project evaluation rubric (page 110) at the beginning of the project, so students will know the evaluation criteria. Students, working in groups of three, will develop the background knowledge to take on a character in a role play. Eventually developing a role-play script as part of this project, each group will dramatize a conversation among three very diverse characters, whose descriptions follow.

Role-Play Characters

- The American frontier explorer of the year 1800, who will be called the "Homespunian" in subsequent text references here—alluding to the homespun fabric worn by early settlers.
- A person of the year 2000, who leads an active lifestyle and will subsequently be called the "Lycranian"—alluding to a modern synthetic fabric such as Lycra.
- A modern-day expert on nutrition, who will be simply be referred to as the "nutritionist."

For this project all three of the role-play characters will be adults between the ages of twenty-five and thirty-five. Acting as a group facilitator, the nutritionist will be responsible for coordinating the overall focus of the role play on the importance of diet in establishing a healthy lifestyle and avoiding chronic disease. The nutritionist will act as an advisor as the other two characters describe their lifestyles, diets, and health problems.

Each member of a group can use his or her creativity to create the designated character. For instance, a student role-playing the Homespunian can decide where the character is living, what the character's daily activities might be, and what the character eats every day. For example, the student will, as that character, be able to describe her overall health, focusing on symptoms of chronic, diet-related diseases she might have. In response, the student role-playing a nutritionist can explain how these symptoms might be diet-related and what dietary changes could result in improved overall health.

Members of the group will meet frequently to plan the role play, discussing among themselves the health implications of the diets of the Lycranian and the Homespunian. As the group progresses through the three stages of the project, each member will become well-versed about the symptoms of chronic disease that might result from the diets of the Lycranian and the Homespunian. The nutritionist of the team will make sure the other two members know which diet choices could delay the onset of such chronic diseases or slow their progress once they have begun.

✳ FIRST-STORY INTELLECT

Gathering Information

Each student will begin the information-gathering activities for this project by *reading* about explorers of the early 1800s, diet and lifestyle of today's society, and the study of nutrition. (Refer to Project Learning Log 1 at the end of the chapter.) To learn about the person of the 1800s, the Homespunian students who are doing first-story intellect work should research and *read* materials about the great American explorers of the 1800s, particularly Meriwether Lewis and George Rogers Clark. The diet of their Corps of Discovery, typical of the diet of frontier-dwellers as well as plains- and mountain-explorers, was very well-documented in the journals of officers and other members of the expedition. Students may want to read portions of those journals, which were published and are generally accessible, to collect information about typical frontier rations and remedies used for illnesses on the trail during the early 1800s.

A book about the Lewis and Clark expedition that is especially useful for this project is *Undaunted Courage* (Ambrose 1996), specifically those sections of the book that describe rations of food for the Lewis and Clark Corps of Discovery. This book also contains information about some of the

homeopathic remedies that were used in the early 1800s and the symptoms of the chronic diseases the remedies alleviated.

To *research* the modern-day person's lifestyle and diet, students should read such books as *Eating on the Run* (Tribole 1991) to learn about the diet and lifestyle of the modern-day person entering the new millennium. Students could also read *Eat Smart: A Guide to Good Health for Kids* (Figtree 1997) to learn about making some healthy eating choices. In researching diet, in general, the students should obtain a copy of the food pyramid, which will be especially useful for the nutritionist of the group.

Students will also *interview* several people who can provide more details about a typical day in the lives of the role-play characters. A history teacher or historical reenactor, or even the librarian/media center director, can offer students insights on what life was like for someone in the Lewis and Clark expedition, or at least point students in the right direction for collecting more information.

To *research* the typical person of today, students may interview family friends who lead busy, active lives or parents who juggle work, home, and personal recreation. These adults can provide many details about what they do and how they eat. A nutritionist or home economics/life sciences or health teacher may be available to help students learn about the connections between careless diet and chronic disease, as well as those between careful diet and health. Students will research the diets of the Homespunian and the Lycranian to determine the vitamins, minerals, and other nutrients contained in the foods eaten by these characters. *Eat Smart,* the book mentioned previously, is one of the sources for this information.

Students may divide interview responsibilities. Groups may determine who interviews whom by which role each group member assumes, rather than by having each member interview people about all three characters in the role play.

Students may also *search the Internet* for information about links between diet and healthy lifestyle. Some addresses to try are http://www.advocatehealth.com/fitness/fittime. html, http://www.lbcommunity.com/family/yhnut.html, and http://www.eatright.ort/mschool-based.html. Students may ask a search engine such as AltaVista, WebCrawler, or Yahoo to look for "diet and health," "positive lifestyle," "food groups," "food pyramid," or "diet and prevention." Students can also try their own phrases to hit as many Web sites as possible.

Students can *view* television programs for more information about growing and preparing food. PBS stations feature programs such as *Victory Garden, Baking with Julia,* and *The Frugal Gourmet.* On cable, The Discovery Channel features *Great Chefs* and offers a Web site at http://www. discovery.com, where students may get more information about programming on The Discovery Channel or The Learning Channel. Another cable

channel, Lifetime, offers a variety of cooking and food shopping programs. Chefs Jeff Smith and Graham Kerr, among others, give information about the healthiness of many of their recipes.

Popular culture can influence eating habits. As students *listen* to favorite radio and television stations, they can keep a notebook handy in which they keep a log of commercials for restaurants, including fast-food eateries. Each log entry will include the name of the restaurant, the date and time that the student heard the commercial, and what food items were featured in the commercial. Students can collect more data by *visiting* these restaurants and asking for nutritional information about the food products that were advertised in the commercials. Many fast-food restaurants such as McDonald's and Burger King have booklets containing this information available for their customers. Students can record this information, including total calories and fat or carbohydrate grams contained in the food products.

Students will also spend some time in a local grocery store getting nutritional information from the labels of at least seven different packaged foods: a breakfast food, a dried pea or bean, a pasta, a frozen vegetable product, and a frozen pizza—plus two more from different categories. Students will get information from products that a typical active person of today might actually use or from products that are representative of what these characters eat.

To research the diets of people in the early nineteenth century, students may investigate the local historical society or a regional museum, which may offer information and perhaps a display on the history of farming and cooking in that particular area. Students will look for historical pictures showing kitchens of the time as well as farms, gardens, restaurants, or other examples of food producers, seeking information about the diet of people who lived in the area in the early 1800s.

For instance, museums will often have information about the diet of Native American tribes indigenous to the particular region. Through investigating the diet of Native Americans in the Great Lakes region of the United States, for example, students will find that they raised some vegetable crops— mainly beans, corn, and some varieties of squash; caught fish such as lake trout and whitefish; hunted deer, moose, and turkeys; and used porcupines as "emergency" food because these animals were so slow-moving that they could always be caught if no other food was available.

✳ SECOND-STORY INTELLECT

Focusing on the Goal: A Role Play

When information has been collected for the Homespunian's and the Lycranian's diets and lifestyles, the planning of a healthy diet, and the impact of diet on general health, students will be ready to begin the second-story intellect phase of the project. (Refer to Project Learning Log 2 at the

end of the chapter.) Each group will begin these *processing* activities by reviewing what members of the group have learned about the Lycranian and the Homespunian and the information that the nutritionist will use to help these characters develop healthier eating habits. Each member of the group will spend some time *processing* the information about his or her character and *developing* that character for the role play.

At the start of the role-playing exercise, the student will name his or her character, describe the character's lifestyle and diet, and develop a health profile for the character that will include at least two symptoms of chronic health problems that are diet-related. Members of the group will meet to discuss the characters. Students who will role-play the Homespunian and the Lycranian will each take a turn describing the characters that they have developed and the diet-related health problems experienced by the characters. The nutritionist will summarize information about a healthy diet using the food pyramid. The group will discuss the chronic health problems experienced by the Homespunian and the Lycranian, the eating habits that contribute to these problems, and the eating choices that can help the characters improve their health.

Illustrating

Each student will *sketch* a costume and name badge for her character in the role play. To plan an appropriate costume, the Homespunian can look at the cover illustrations of books he or she has resesarched as well as pictures from the historical society museum or U.S. history textbooks. The Lycranian will use information from clothing ads that he or she sees in the newspaper or suggestions from a parent or other adult who leads a busy lifestyle to design a contemporary costume. The nutritionist may be able to borrow a lab coat or jacket from the science or photography department to wear over contemporary, professional-person clothing—clothing a businessperson might wear to the office. Each student may want to revisit the person who was interviewed to get background information about the character and to ask for feedback about the planned costume. For example, the student can ask this person for suggestions on how to improve the costume so that it helps her portray the character as accurately as possible.

Using a fishbone or a grid, each student will *diagram* the activities that the selected character would do in a day. The student will identify the type of activity—sitting, doing office work, walking, running, paddling a canoe, gardening, chopping wood, doing aerobic exercise, and sleeping are some examples—and the number of hours (or minutes) spent doing that activity. The teacher will give each student a chart that shows how many calories are burned per pound of body weight by doing certain activities for given amounts of time. With the information from such a chart, a student may *calculate* the number of calories a given character in the role play would burn in one day.

In addition, each student will obtain a chart that shows how many calories are contained in given portions of a variety of foods. Health or life sciences/home economics teachers can direct students to this information. Each student will then calculate the number of calories that are contained in the food that a role-play character would eat in one day, as well as the percentage of calories that character would burn in one day, deciding whether the character would maintain, lose, or gain weight given the amount of food eaten and the number of calories burned. Each student can use this information to decide if obesity may be one of the chronic health problems experienced by the role-play character, or if that character may experience weight loss and loss of muscle or bone mass because the character uses more calories than he or she eats. Students will include the results of these calculations as part of the activity diagrams for the characters.

Generating a Mini-Biography of a Character

The group will meet again to share information about the characters and their health. The Homespunian and the Lycranian will ask the nutritionist if he or she understands very clearly what physical symptoms of careless eating they are describing for their characters and what chronic illnesses may be indicated by these symptoms. All three members of the group will participate in planning the advice that the nutritionist will offer to teammates about making healthier eating choices.

After this meeting, students will *generate* written mini-biographies for their characters. Each student will include information that will help the character come alive for an audience. The student should describe the character's likes and dislikes, goals and dreams, home and family background, education or other training, and experiences that led the character to where he or she is today. The student will also include the information that she developed earlier about the character's daily lifestyle and eating habits. In addition to being a reference for the role-play preparation, the mini-biographies will be used as a resource at the presentation stage of the project, for which the group will be expected to write a playbill.

Developing Prototypes

The groups will meet again so that students can share the mini-biographies with each other. Then each group will *develop a prototype* for its role play in the form of an outline of the general course of the three-way discussion. (The script will be developed from this outline.) The group will decide who starts the discussion. It may start, for example, with the Lycranian and the Homespunian visiting the nutritionist in her office. The nutritionist may begin the dialogue by welcoming the others to her office and asking them what brought them to visit her. One of the others may answer that she is there because her doctor decided that she needed some help in finding

healthier ways to eat. The nutritionist could ask this person to describe her lifestyle and eating habits.

As an example, in the course of describing her lifestyle to the nutritionist, the Lycranian might mention symptoms of health problems that could be related to poor diet. For instance, heartburn may be a result of eating too fast and eating high-fat foods. Feeling tired may result from a diet that is low in complex carbohydrates. Fatigue may also result from a diet that is high in refined sugar "treats."

As another example, the Homespunian might mention mouth sores and loose teeth, due to what the nutritionist may tell him is a lack of vitamin C in his diet. Members of the group will refer to a list of symptoms related to such dietary problems, which they will have gleaned from earlier discussions.

At this stage of the project, teammates will make final decisions about who has what symptoms so they can prepare the role-play script. Members of the group may also decide that after the Homespunian has given his or her information, the Lycranian will jump into the discussion with similar lifestyle and diet data.

Scripting the Role Play

The group will develop a script for the role play, including dialogue tags indicating who is speaking. The group will want to decide on ground rules for improvisation during the role play—for times when inspiration strikes and a teammate wants to depart from the outline. For instance, the group can decide how a member can signal the others that she wants to add something unplanned to the role play. They may also want to agree on how to help each other out during the performance of the role play. If the Homespunian announces he has mouth sores and loose teeth, for instance, and the nutritionist momentarily forgets that the disease associated with these symptoms is called scurvy, the Homespunian could cue her. He could "ad-lib" dialogue not in the script, such as "I think I remember hearing about a disease called scurvy. Could that be my problem?"

At this point, members of the group will decide on the title for their role play and will pick a song and rewrite the lyrics to say something about healthy eating. This song would be the finale to the role-play presentation. If a group picks "Row, row, row your boat," the new lyrics may be, "Food can be your pal—veggies, fruit, and meat—pasta, dairy, bread, and fish—help to keep you well."

Instead of doing a song, some groups may decide to rewrite a poem, such as Carl Sandburg's "The Fog," to sound something like this: "We can eat/to maintain good health./We eat veggies/carbos, dairy, and meat/in balanced amounts/and not much junk." A group could recite the poem as the finale for its role-play performance.

✳ THIRD-STORY INTELLECT

Testing, Showcasing, and Evaluating

Each group will begin the third-story intellect activities by doing a run-through of the role-play script to *try* it out. (Refer to Project Learning Log 3 at the end of the chapter.) One member of the group will watch the time, a second person will encourage everyone in the group to "stick close to the script," and the third group member will keep the discussion moving by intervening if a teammate seems to be getting long-winded. Each member of the group will have a notebook open and will jot down notes about what he or she likes and what could be improved. Members of the group will discuss this run-through with each other, agree on improvements, and do a second run-through to smooth out the rough spots.

Each group will then do a dress rehearsal of its role play for a feedback group. On a day announced by the teacher, students will bring their costumes to class for rehearsal, with the teacher allowing time for dressing. Each group will be partnered with a feedback group. Each group will do its role play for its corresponding feedback group. Members of the feedback group will jot down quick notes telling what they liked about the role play, what they thought was strong, and what they thought needed clarification. A group will begin the feedback by telling the other group what it liked about the role play and what it thought the stronger parts were—before talking about the weaker parts. After both groups have given their feedback, they will thank each other for the help.

Revising and Assessing

Each group will use the feedback to *revise* its role play. The group will use the feedback comments to clarify and expand the role play. For instance, suppose that the feedback from the observing group members was that they did not really understand why the Lycranian was very tired around 2:30 every afternoon. The role-play group might look at its script and decide that the Lycranian needs to emphasize in the script that she always eats a large dish of ice cream for lunch. The group will also note the nutritionist will then suggest to the Lycranian that she is experiencing a blood sugar "crash" brought on by her high-sugar lunch and that a lunch that includes some raw vegetables, a bagel, a small portion of cheese, and some fruit might give the Lycranian a more stable, consistent energy level through the afternoon. Requests for clarification probably mean that the role play needs different wording of a line or some elaboration.

When the rewrites of the role-play script are done, the groups will meet again. Each group will perform the rewritten scenes in its role play while the other group takes notes. The groups will again exchange feedback. Each group will take the feedback that it gets and do a fine-tuning of its role-play outline.

Showcasing

The showcasing phase of the project involves the performance of the role play, the final presentation of the project. As part of preparation for the performance, each group of students will create a playbill for its role play, which will be photocopied and given to the audience. Drawing from the role-play script, the playbill will carry the role-play title and will include brief biographies of the characters. The characters' activities, eating habits, and chronic health problems will be included.

For instance, a group might include the following description of a character in the playbill for its role play:

> Sairy O'Shea, Homespunian—chops wood, fishes, hunts bear, tends a large garden, does laundry with a washboard and lye soap, hauls water from a well—eats some vegetables from the garden, meat and fish that she catches or shoots—winter diet is almost all dried meat and fish—by spring has sore, bleeding gums and loose teeth—may be scurvy due to lack of vitamin C in winter diet.

The playbill will also contain advice that the nutritionist may give to help with the problem: "Sairy can preserve some garden greens in a root cellar to supplement her winter diet. She may also eat raw bear grease—this may contain high levels of vitamin C." The group may also include a sketch of each character and a diagram of the food guide pyramid in the playbill. The text in the playbill will be done using a word processor. The sketches will be done with dark-colored markers so they will photocopy well.

Each group may *perform* its role play not only for the class itself, but also—possibly—for another class in the school that is learning about the United States in the early 1800s, for a drama class or for a health class, depending on arrangements the teacher is able to make.

On the performance date, each group should be prepared to get into costume before the presentation time, be ready to explain the background of the role play, perform the role play, hand out the playbills, and sing its nutrition song or recite its poem. The audience class will *celebrate* success with the group by using applause or some other energizer.

After a performance, the audience members may be prompted to brainstorm

- A list of three symptoms of chronic disease that may be linked to unhealthy eating, which they learned from the role play.
- Two suggestions about healthy eating that members of the audience class want to remember.
- One memorable moment from the role play.

The teacher or some appointee from the audience-class may create a "thank-you" card for the role-play group, featuring a summary of the follow-up/brainstorming session. Each member of the audience-class may then sign the thank-you card before it is delivered to the role-play group.

Each student will assemble an *individual portfolio* for the project that includes the notes from the interview that provided some background information and details; the radio/television log of fast-food commercials; the fast-food nutritional information; the design sketches for the character's costume and badge; the diagram showing the character's daily activity; the calculations of calories eaten and burned by the character in a day, the predictions about diet-related chronic health problems that the character might experience; and the mini-biography of the character.

Each group will also compile a *project portfolio* that contains the rough draft of the role-play script with critique notes; the final role-play script; the rough draft of the playbill with written comments from a feedback group; a copy of the final playbill; and the thank-you card if the group received one from the audience. The teacher may have these group portfolios on display in the classroom after the project's completion.

Self-Evaluation and Group Evaluation

In addition to using the rubric, students will self-evaluate by writing assessments of their project work and performance in their journals.

Students may reflect on the following questions:

- What are two specific facts or ideas that you learned about how a healthy diet can help you avoid chronic disease?

- How will you apply these ideas to your life?

- What did you do well as you organized information and created your character for the role play? What is one organizational skill that you learned that will help you in the future?

- As you learned and presented information in this project by reading, writing, diagramming, calculating, organizing, role-playing, singing, working on a team, and working alone, when did you feel the most comfortable? When did you feel the least comfortable? How do you think you can improve your comfort level?

Group work, an integral part of the project, will be addressed as well. As a closure activity, teammates will reflect on their performance as a whole and reach conclusions about what they learned through teamwork.

Teammates will assess their group performance and knowledge gained through the project by discussing the following:

- What three differences between the diets of the Homespunian and the Lycranian do we find most interesting? What are our reasons for picking these differences?

- What two similarities in their diets do we find the most interesting? What are our reasons for these choices?

- What one piece of nutritional knowledge would we most like to pass along? Why did we pick this piece of knowledge?

- How well did we "tug at ideas, not people" to reach consensus on the answers to the previous questions? What were our best strategies? What do we want to improve the next time we work as a team?

The entire class will *celebrate* successful completion of the project and their new nutritional savvy by eating a healthy snack together and doing a group cheer.

Project Evaluation Rubric
Chapter 7: Are You What You Eat?

Performance / Criteria	0	1	2	3
Balance of roles in role-play script	Roles not balanced; one character dominates	Roles not balanced; two characters overshadow the third	Roles balanced for most of the play	Roles consistently well balanced throughout play
Costuming of characters	No costuming	Some costuming; somewhat inconsistent with characters	Generally appropriate costuming	Accurate costuming from head to toe
Information on characters in playbill	No information on characters other than name	Information for one of three characters	Information for two or three characters	Complete information for all three characters
Quality of role-play performance	Mumbling and stumbling through the play	Some non sequiturs; some forgetfulness	Performance smooth most of the time	Bravo!
Song/poem about nutritional learning	No information about nutrition included; not "in beat"	Some information included; not "in beat"	Some information included; "in beat" most of the time	Standing ovation!

SkyLight Training and Publishing, Inc.

Project Learning Log 1

✹ **First-Story Intellect: Gathering Information**

Describe what you did to gather information.

- **Read**

....

....

....

- **Visited**

....

....

....

- **Researched**

....

....

....

- **Interviewed**

....

....

....

- **Surfed the 'Net**

....

....

....

- **And . . .**

....

....

Project Learning Log 2

✸ **Second-Story Intellect: Processing Information**

Describe what you did to process information.

- **Sketched**

....

....

....

- **Analyzed**

....

....

....

- **Calculated/Graphed**

....

....

....

- **Developed Prototypes**

....

....

....

- **Drew**

....

....

....

- **And . . .**

....

....

Project Learning Log 3
✳ Third-Story Intellect: Applying Information

Describe what you did to apply information.

- **Tried/Tested**

....
....
....

- **Evaluated**

....
....
....

- **Revised**

....
....
....

- **Repeated the Cycle**

....
....
....

- **Showcased**

....
....
....

- **And . . .**

....
....

Chapter 8

Designing a Better Shopping Cart

An Applied Technology Project

Most students have had experience with shopping carts in grocery, discount, and toy stores. They may be well aware of some of the problems that customers encounter, such as one wheel of the cart getting stuck in position, making it difficult to steer. As they do this project, students will learn what consumers do and do not like about present shopping carts and what improvements these consumers would like to see. Students will do field research to obtain this information and learn about various types of shopping carts. Analyzing the information they gather and deciding what is "user-friendly" about present shopping-cart design, they will collaborate on the design and building of their own prototype shopping carts.

This is a *template project*. All shopping carts—or go-karts, tea carts, baby strollers, or golf carts—are built around a common form or pattern or structure (a template) that includes a platform which can hold some weighty objects, wheels that are used to move the platform, a power source to move the platform (an energy source such as a battery or a person who can push), restraining sides to keep objects from falling off of the platform, and a steering mechanism that can be used to change the direction in which the platform is moving. At the start of this project, the teacher may distribute the project evaluation rubric (page 127) so students will know the evaluation criteria.

As students begin work on this project, they can be creative about the materials that they use, about the shape of the cart, whether to make single-level or multilevel carts, and whether each level of the cart will have a single compartment or several compartments. Students will have the flexibility to decide how simple or complex to make the steering mechanism, whether the carts will be propelled by a person or a motor, whether to make rigid or flexible carts, and so on. However, prototypes will need to include a platform, wheels, sides, a direction-changing mechanism, and a power source—those items being the template elements that define a shopping cart.

This is a good project for groups of four students, each of whom will be assigned to or will choose a specific role.

Shopping-Cart Design Team Roles

- The project manager, who keeps the group focused (on schedule) and assigns individual responsibilities.

- The materials coordinator, who collects the supplies that are needed to build the prototype and makes sure that the group has all of the supplies available each time it meets.

- The construction engineer, who assigns the responsibilities for building different parts of the prototype and supervises final assembly of the prototype.

- The creations specialist, who encourages the team to develop creative solutions to shopping-cart design and leads energizer breaks and celebrations at the end of each work session.

✳ FIRST-STORY INTELLECT

Gathering Information

Each group will begin its first-story intellect information gathering by doing some field *research.* (Refer to Project Learning Log 1 at the end of the chapter.) Each team will plan on testing at least three different carts in three different stores that it visits. The project manager will set up appointments at three area stores where the team has received permission to do the field testing.

To make such arrangements, the individual will telephone the managers of several area stores where shopping carts are used. The individual will introduce himself or herself as a student, briefly explain the project and the field-testing process as described in this section (including the interviewing of customers), and then ask for permission to do the field-testing portion of the project at that respective store. Arrangements may be made for the testing to be done during regular shopping hours or after the store closes. The student will be ready to provide an adult chaperone if the manager requests that a parent, teacher, or other adult supervisor accompany the group to the store. The teacher may choose to coordinate this phase of the project for the teams.

For the field test, each team will take a notebook in which the creations specialist of the team will observe and record the results of the visit, keeping a chart or notes about what the team does with the cart and whether the individual members liked the way the cart worked. Throughout this field-testing phase of the project, group members will verbalize their observations so the assigned specialist can record the data. The specialist will begin by logging what happens when the team members enter a store and get a cart from the cart pick-up area. At this point the following questions should be addressed:

- How easy it is to get the cart separated from others in a group or row?
- Can the cart be pulled away from others using the handle and backing the cart out of the row? Or is the cart pulled away from the front of the row?
- How easily can the cart be steered as it is pulled out of the cart pickup?
- Does someone need to turn the cart around to get it headed in the direction that the team wants to go? If so, how easy it is to turn the cart around?
- Where is the child-seat located in the cart and how does it operate? If a team member has to fold the seat up, does it stay closed or does it fall open when not in use?

As part of the field test, the team will make arrangements—with permission—to take a small child, perhaps a younger brother or sister of one of the teammates, to at least one of the stores. The team will practice putting the child into and taking the child out of the child-seat of a shopping cart, noting how easy or awkward it is to do so.

As another part of the field test, the team will practice loading and unloading a large, heavy item such as a forty-pound bag of dog food or a forty-pound block or bag of rock salt. Team members will place the heavy item on the bottom rack of the cart, observing how easy it was to get the item onto the cart and then get it back off.

Next, the team will practice loading and unloading several medium-sized and small-sized objects from each cart, objects such as boxes of cereal, cans of vegetables or soup, five-pound bags of sugar or flour, small cans or bottles of spices, a toothbrush or package of dental floss, or a box of toothpicks. As the experimenting continues, the team will also practice loading soft items such as bread or napkins with hard items such as cans or bottles. In the log, the specialist will be sure to record the appearance of the soft item before loading it into the cart as well as its appearance later.

Each teammate will steer carts through the most crowded, narrow aisles that can be found, recording how easy it is to avoid hitting objects or other shoppers—who will be role-played by fellow teammates. In addition, students will test how easy it is to steer carts around corners as well as how easy the carts are to steer when they are lightly loaded and, later, heavily loaded.

As another step in the field test, teammates will practice steering loaded carts into checkout lines, taking the items out of the carts, placing the individual items on the counter, and reloading the cart with bagged items, observing how smoothly or awkwardly they can do each step of the unloading and reloading operation. For example, a teammate will note whether she unloaded the cart from the front, the side, or the back and her reason for choosing that point for unloading. Depending upon the arrangements made with the store manager and how mcuh time the students have to use the checkout counter, students may be able to repeat this process several times.

If the project manager obtained permission from the store manager to *interview* other shoppers to learn what they do and do not like about current shopping-cart design, the team will select at random at least twelve adult shoppers who are leaving the store with cartfuls of purchases. Students will introduce themselves and ask the shopper to take the following brief survey:

Customer Survey

- How easy or awkward was it for you to

    separate a shopping cart from others in a row?

    get the cart going the direction you want it to go?

    get a child into and out of the child-seat?

    load a heavy item onto the bottom rack?

    unload a heavy item?

    steer through the aisles?

    turn corners?

    unload the cart at the checkout counter?

    get the cart out of the store?

- Which feature of the shopping cart do you find most helpful?
- Which feature would you most like to change?

Each group will design a questionnaire based on these questions and include spaces in which the interviewer will indicate the approximate age of each person interviewed, the person's gender, and whether the person was short, of average height, or tall.

If a store manager did not give permission for students to interview customers on store premises, perhaps feeling that shoppers will be annoyed or inconvenienced, members of the team will—at a later time and off store premises—approach people they know who frequent that particular establishment and ask them to take the survey. In any case, the team will collect interview results from at least twelve adult shoppers.

SkyLight Training and Publishing, Inc.

When the team visits the stores to field-test the shopping carts, each teammate will *watch* shoppers actually using carts and record those observations. (Teammates will play the role of other shoppers if the store manager has asked the team to come in at a time when other customers are not present.) Each teammate will pay particular attention to others as they take corners, steer their carts through narrow aisles, and avoid head-on collisions. Group members will also note how a shopper places items in the basket portion as well as on the bottom rack of the cart, recording any problems they see. At the checkout line, students will observe how easily or awkwardly a shopper removes items from the basket and the bottom rack, making note of such problems as a shorter customer having trouble reaching items at the bottom of the cart.

Students will *sketch* or *photograph* each shopping cart that they use. The sketch or photo will provide the visual data that students need to decide what physical dimensions of shopping carts are good and what might need to be changed when the students begin to create their new designs. Students will also *listen* for sounds that indicate a problem with cart wheels. Squeaking, vibrating, or rattling noises are sounds that can tell students about lack of wheel lubrication, balance, and the effects of extended use.

Shopping carts have much in common with some pieces of home furniture such as baby cribs, playpens, tea carts, kitchen-storage caddies, or microwave-oven carts. Students may also choose to look at plans for baby buggies and strollers. They may want to visit a toy or discount store to inspect and make notes on the steering mechanisms for strollers or buggies. To learn more about design, students will *read* such resources as *Toys, Games and Furniture (The Family Handyman)* (Reader's Digest 1995), and *Furniture by Design: Design, Construction and Technique* (Blackburn 1997).

Students can *search the Internet* to learn more about carts or to get ideas about some of the simple machines that can be used in cart construction—items such as wheels, levers, and pulleys. Students may find information about grocery carts at http://www.walkincooler.com/cart. Information about designing carts for carrying loads is available at http://www.soc.plym.ac.uk/EFAE/efaedemo/3D/3design. HTM, and at http://www.nbbd.com/golfcar/utility. Both of these addresses provide links for students to follow. Students may also use search engines such as AltaVista or WebCrawler, using the key words "grocery carts," "golf carts," "go-karts," or "simple machines." Searching for "shopping carts" on the Internet may result in a large number of unproductive sites for purposes of this project. So many shopping services offer "on-line shopping carts" for their customers that browsers will find many "shopping cart" references lead to these on-line stores or to Web sites targeted to the design of cyberspace carts.

✳ SECOND-STORY INTELLECT

Focusing on the Goal: A New Shopping-Cart Design

Students will move into *processing* activities associated with the second-story intellect by meeting in their assigned design groups to *organize* and *analyze* the information that was collected during the field test. (Refer to Project Learning Log 2 at the end of the chapter.) Students will organize the data or information about shopping carts in the grid (a graphic organizer) that follows.

Qualities / Cart Features	Current Design	Positive/ Helpful	Negative/ Awkward	Keep/ Redesign
Platform				
Wheels				
Power Source				
Sides				
Steering				

Information about the current design of shopping carts will be recorded in the first column on the grid. Students will record data from the field-test log using this organizer, sorting out the design pros and cons of the carts that were tested. Although the group will indicate whether to keep a design feature or to reengineer that feature for its prototype cart, the group will not be working on its design at this point. There will be time for that later.

In filling out the grid, students will note that a single design feature may have both positive and negative qualities. For example, one power source for the cart, "a person pushing" as opposed to a battery-operated system, is considered a positive in that the person pushing does not take up space in the cart. The negative of that power source might be that a fully loaded cart will require strenuous pushing, which may be difficult for a person to do.

The group members may decide that the "person pushing" is a power source for which the positives outweigh the negatives, so they will note on their grid that this feature will be kept when they design their cart.

As another illustration, the steering system of a certain cart may be "front wheels that turn without a steering column." As the students sort information on the grid, they may record that this feature is helpful in keeping cart design simple. However, the group may also note that the feature is awkward because it requires the person who is pushing to know exactly how to exert leverage to turn the front end of the cart, that is, to get the steering wheels to turn. The students may then decide that this feature is so awkward that they want to redesign the steering system.

Brainstorming and Generating a New Cart Design

Once the information from the field test is organized, the group will go back through the last column of the grid, identify the cart features that group members want to redesign, and begin to brainstorm ways to improve shopping-cart design. If the group decides to redesign the steering, for example, one of the members might suggest that they could use a steering system like bicycle handles. Then another member of the group might suggest that bicycle handles be attached directly to the front wheels of the cart. This could lead to a discussion of whether to redesign carts so that shoppers pull the carts rather than push them.

As brainstorming continues, the group may decide that larger wheels with a single turning wheel in front would lead to smoother cornering. The group could then discuss whether using a single wheel might compromise the stability of the cart, especially when it is fully loaded. A short member of the group may argue for lower sides on a cart. Teammates may point out that lower sides would reduce the capacity of the cart. Another member of the group might suggest that the group could design a trap door into the back of the cart. The door could be hinged to swing down to allow for easier access when the shopper is unloading the cart. That could lead to a discussion of what kind of latch would be best and whether such a latch might open accidentally.

During a brainstorming session a group member might suggest that the bottom shelf on a cart be put on gliders or rollers, much like the rollers that are used on the bottom portions of bureau or desk drawers. That way the bottom shelf could be pulled out for easier access when loading or unloading. The group might then discuss how to design such a roller system so that it could support heavy loads, such as forty-pound bags of dog food, which are typically placed on the lower shelf of a cart.

Members of the group will use the redesign ideas from the brainstorm to *generate* two or three designs for improved shopping carts. Teammates will look over the specific design features that the group decided could be used and decide on the five basic elements of their carts, referring to the template for the project.

Template Elements of the Shopping Cart

- Platform
- Steering mechanism
- Set of wheels
- Restraining sides
- Power source

When the group has identified the features that it wants to use in one redesigned cart, it will go back through its list of suggested improvements and develop two more new designs. The group will analyze the designs and pick the one that it likes best following up by writing a short rationale explaining its reasons for choosing one design over the other two.

Illustrating

The group will then *sketch* its new design. The project manager will read the specifications aloud; the materials coordinator will check to be sure that all group members understand each feature of the new design and ask for clarification if they do not. Then the construction engineer will check for agreement by asking questions such as the following: Is that what everyone thought that we meant by this improvement during the brainstorming session? Do we still agree that this is a good idea? Do we want to change or modify our idea?

The creations specialist will then sketch the design on newsprint or sketching paper. The other members of the group may review and assist, determining labels for the various features of the redesigned cart and finalizing functions as well as improvement ideas for these features.

Calculating Volume and Cost

The group will use the dimensions of a present shopping cart to *calculate* its volume. The group will then use the dimensions of its redesigned cart to determine the volume of the new cart. The group will compare the volumes and tell why the new volume is preferable to the old. If the new cart holds more than the old, the group may say that a larger cart is better because shoppers can buy more and make fewer trips to the store. If the new cart holds less than the old, the group could say that a smaller cart is easier to maneuver and push.

Each group will use the design specifications of its cart to *calculate* the cost of making its cart. If the group is making the cart in an applied technology or industrial arts class, the teacher can give the group "shop prices" of materials that are available for purchase through the school. If the project is done in a department other than applied technology or industrial arts, the teacher will be prepared to give the students advice about how to obtain materials and where to build the prototypes.

Supplying and purchasing materials for the project can be handled in various ways. One idea is to look for old baby strollers, bicycles, and other items that can be "salvaged" for cart parts at garage sales. Parents will be approached ahead of time if students will be expected to pay for materials. Another option is to find sponsors, such as parent-teacher groups, who will be willing to help pay for some of the materials for this project. A class may publicize the project and offer to sell the carts, at cost, to interested purchasers; the class may even decide to hold a raffle. Another option is to approach the stores that cooperated in the field-testing part of the project, who may want to buy the experimental carts as a goodwill gesture or at least help defray project cost. An interested parent/teacher group may also agree to help students with expenses. In any case, how the project will be financed will be determined ahead of time.

To help with calculation, the teacher will give students information about the prices of shopping carts that stores presently use. The teacher may gather this information from the managers of the stores that cooperated in the field-testing, from one of the Web sites mentioned earlier in this chapter, or from a supplier's catalog. Each group will compare the price of its redesigned cart with the prices of actual store carts.

Creating a Promotional Brochure

Each group will *design* a brochure that could be used to sell its shopping carts to businesses. The group will design a cover that features a group logo. For example, a logo may be designed showing four people proudly displaying the redesigned cart that is full of consumer goods. The information inside of the brochure will include cart specifications, a sketch of the new cart, and a comparison of the new cart with present ones to show why the new cart is more user-friendly.

The brochure will include stick-figure *drawings* that compare and contrast consumers loading or unloading present shopping carts as well as the improved shopping cart, emphasizing advantages of using the new cart. Each group will make a presentation copy of its brochure, doing the text with a word processor and the illustrations as black line drawings so that the brochure is "photocopiable." The group will plan on making photocopies for each member of the class and the teacher in preparation for "final presentation."

Developing Prototypes

To complete the information processing, each group will *build a prototype* of its redesigned cart. This will be a working prototype of the redesigned cart in which all parts must operate as they will in the production model of the cart. If financing or in-school technology is not available to build a model like production models (actual store carts), the groups may build scale models of the prototypes by using substitute parts, such as wheels from a baby stroller instead of the heavy-duty wheels on most shopping carts.

If the group is doing this project for an applied technology or industrial arts/shop course, materials and shop equipment may be available through the school. Otherwise, members of the team may need to go back to the stores where they priced materials to buy some of the shopping-cart components that they need for the prototype. In any case, the materials coordinator of each group will make sure that the group has all of the materials needed to build the prototype, working within the parameters established at the beginning of the project.

✳ THIRD-STORY INTELLECT

Testing, Showcasing, and Evaluating

The group will move into third-story intellect activities by trying out its cart to see how it works. (Refer to Project Learning Log 3 at the end of the chapter.) The group will push the cart around the shop area, garage, or workroom where they built it. Teammates will check the prototype cart's steering, cornering, and ease of pushing or pulling.

If team members can obtain permission to go back to a cooperating store to test their prototype cart, assuming their cart is designed to withstand a real-world test, students will try procedures they used during the first phase of the project—checking their results against the log from their first store visit. In any case, whether testing is done on or off store premises, students will answer the questions below:

- Is this cart easier to push and steer than the cart that you usually use in this store?
- Is it easier to load and unload?
- How do you like the pull-out bottom shelf?
- Would you use this cart regularly if it were available?

Revising and Assessing

Group members will take their test data and *evaluate* the performance of their shopping cart. The group will use the test data to decide which design features worked well and which features need improvement, deciding whether the redesigned cart is better than present carts or just different from them. Remembering that its job is to design a better shopping cart, the group will *redesign* the prototype cart features that did not test well and *rebuild* the prototype. The group will put this rebuilt prototype through the testing process and evaluate the new field-test data. The group will have its shopping cart ready to demonstrate to the class by the project deadline.

The group will assemble its project *portfolio.* The portfolio will include the following: the notes from the initial field-testing of existing shopping carts; the completed questionnaires from the interviews with adult shoppers; the sketches or photos of the store carts that were tested with a description of any troublesome noises made by each cart; the graphic organizer or grid of information; the preliminary sketches for new cart designs; the cart volume and cost calculations; sketches or photos of the original prototype and the final cart; the evaluation of the prototype with suggestions for improvement; and one copy of the sales brochure. Each group will display the portfolio in its shopping cart at the conclusion of the project.

Showcasing the Project

The group will *showcase* its shopping cart by demonstrating the rebuilt prototype shopping cart to the class. Each group will show the class how its cart steers and pushes or pulls and ask a few volunteers from the class to give the cart a short trial. The group will explain the differences between present carts and the prototype to the class. The group will go over its prototype feature by feature and tell the class why the prototype is easier to use. Finally, the group will give each classmate and the teacher a copy of the sales brochure to study as the group goes through the demonstration and explanation.

The class will *celebrate* success with each group by applauding or using some other appropriate demonstration of appreciation when the group is finished with its presentation.

Self-Evaluation and Group Evaluation

In addition to using the rubric, students will write self-assessments on their project learnings and performances.

> In their journals, students will complete the following sentences:
>
> - As I did this project, two of my important learnings about doing field research were . . .
> - Two ideas I want to remember about analyzing research data are . . .
> - I believe my group used creative design processes well when we . . .

To assess group performance, each team will meet to discuss the various responses to the self-assessment activity. They will take time to discuss and then record their colleagues' answers. The group will then assess the techniques they used as a whole to design and build the prototype, deciding what was strong about their performance as well as what they would do

differently. Also, they will address how or if using different techniques could improve overall group performance. As closure, the group will complete this analogy: Designing a better shopping cart is like <u>(name an action adventure)</u> because both have <u>(name two features)</u> in common.

Finally, the group members will *celebrate* successful completion of the project by writing their completed analogy on a long strip of newsprint or posterboard, signing the work, and using it to decorate the prototype shopping cart on display.

Project Evaluation Rubric
Chapter 8: Designing a Better Shopping Cart

Performance / Criteria	0	1	2	3
Information grid (analysis of shopping cart in store)	No category or just one category analyzed in detail	Two categories analyzed in detail	Three categories analyzed in detail	All four categories analyzed in detail
Sketch of assembly and design features of redesigned shopping cart	Cart cannot be built using these plans	Cart builder will need help using plans at least four times	Cart builder will need help using plans two or three times	Cart builder will need help no more than once
Prediction of advantages of the new shopping cart	No advantages or one advantage predicted	Two advantages predicted	Three advantages predicted	Four or more advantages predicted
Sales brochure for new shopping cart	Addresses no features or just one or two features	Addresses only three features completely	Addresses only four features completely	Addresses all five features completely
Test of advantages of new shopping cart	No advantages tested or one advantage tested	Only two advantages tested	Only three advantages tested	At least four advantages tested

Project Learning Log 1

✳ First-Story Intellect: Gathering Information

Describe what you did to gather information.

- **Read**

....

....

....

- **Visited**

....

....

....

- **Researched**

....

....

....

- **Interviewed**

....

....

....

- **Surfed the 'Net**

....

....

....

- **And . . .**

....

....

SkyLight Training and Publishing, Inc.

Project Learning Log 2

✳ **Second-Story Intellect: Processing Information**

Describe what you did to process information.

- **Sketched**

....
....
....

- **Analyzed**

....
....
....

- **Calculated/Graphed**

....
....
....

- **Developed Prototypes**

....
....
....

- **Drew**

....
....
....

- **And . . .**

....
....

Project Learning Log 3

✳ **Third-Story Intellect: Applying Information**

Describe what you did to apply information.

- **Tried/Tested**

....

....

....

- **Evaluated**

....

....

....

- **Revised**

....

....

....

- **Repeated the Cycle**

....

....

....

- **Showcased**

....

....

....

- **And . . .**

....

....

....

SkyLight Training and Publishing, Inc.

Chapter 9

Writing a Children's Science Book

A Science/Language Arts Project

This project requires students to master one bit of science content well enough to be able to collaborate on and produce a children's book on that scientific concept. Students may choose from a vast array of topics, keeping in mind that they will have to simplify text on the topic so it will be understood by a young child.

For example, earth science students may want to explain how caves dissolve out of rock, why volcanoes erupt where they do, what forces and frictions cause earthquakes, or why tornadoes "twist" out of the clouds. Physics students might discuss Newton's laws of motion, how sound and light waves travel, the difference between matter and energy, or the images formed by differently shaped mirrors. Chemistry students may choose to explain the differences among elements; compounds and mixtures; the properties of elementary atomic particles and their arrangement in atoms; how the properties of a specific compound such as water are related to molecular shape; or the differences in molecular motion among solids, liquids, and gases. Biology students might choose to explain the carbon dioxide cycle, the double-helix structure of DNA, photosynthesis, or the genetics behind a physical trait such as eye color.

Students will be assigned to groups and each group will settle on a specific scientific topic for their children's book. As they begin the project, they will collect and organize information about their selected topic, deciding which concepts to include and which grade level (between kindergarten and fourth grade) to target. At this point, the teacher may distribute the project evaluation rubric (page 141), so students will know the evaluation criteria.

This activity is a *genre-related project*. Juvenile literature has set parameters. Students will peruse a few children's general interest books, storybooks, and science books (such as Seymour Simon's science books for children), which they will find in the children's section of the library or the corresponding juvenile section of a bookstore. The students can find

creative ways to teach young children about the topic and to design the layout and illustrations for the book. However, they will follow a standard format as follows.

Components of a Children's Book

- Front and back cover illustrations that tell something about the story.
- A small amount of text on any one page.
- Text written at an age-appropriate level and set in large font size.
- A picture that illustrates the text on each page.
- A "story line" that moves the reader along from page to page, such as a character trying to find a solution to a problem.
- Characters who are interesting to young readers, such as children, animals, cartoon representations, or personified concepts (such as Adam Atom).
- Illustrations—large and colorful—that are attractive to young readers.

This project can be done very effectively by groups or teams of four. The teacher may make group assignments at this time, allowing the members to choose their individual roles from the list below.

Each group for the children's science book project will include

- An editor/accuracy authority, who keeps the group on task and on time and double-checks science content for accuracy.
- An author, who works the scientific concept and process into text targeted to young readers.
- An illustrator, who does the pencil sketches of the illustrations for the book.
- A production coordinator, who is in charge of materials needed and the final assembly of the product (the children's science book).

Each group will identify a teacher of its targeted grade level who may be willing to participate in the project. After the group identifies that cooperating teacher, perhaps one within the school district at a neighboring school, the production coordinator or some other member of the group will contact

that teacher to ask if she or he is available. That "partner/teacher" will be asked to read the rough draft of the science book to identify language that his or her students may not comprehend; help the writing group find age-appropriate vocabulary to communicate its topic to the young readers; use the finished children's science book to teach a science lesson to his or her class; and collect feedback about the lesson from the young students to give to the group. In addition, the cooperating teacher will also give feedback on the book, such as what was strong about the science lesson taught in the book and what revisions could strengthen a future edition.

In situations where it may not be practical for students to personally arrange for cooperating primary school partner/teachers, the project teacher may telephone the principals of nearby elementary schools several weeks before beginning the project, explain the project, and ask the principals to publicize the opportunity to teachers of primary grades. Willing teachers could then be identified. A few days before beginning the project with the class, the project teacher could get the names of the volunteers and write each name on a note card. The production coordinator from each group would then draw a name to learn the identity of that group's partner/teacher for the project.

At this initial stage of the project, the teacher may "kick off" the project by asking student groups to recall what storytime was like in the lower grades. For instance, she may start the remembrances by asking students if their primary school teacher sat in a rocking chair while the children sat on a rug on the floor; if the teacher just read the story aloud or if he or she stopped after each page to show the pictures to the children, asking them to guess what might happen next; how the teacher used posture and voice to suggest changes in characters and mood; and what kind of discussion the class had after the story reading was complete.

As a follow-up or alternative, the teacher may read aloud from a humorous book that is a take-off on a familiar children's story, such as *The Three Little Wolves and the Big Bad Pig* (Trivizas and Oxenbury 1993), using techniques typical of storytellers at the primary level. Students will enjoy a twist on an old story, such as this one. When the teacher is finished reading the book to the class, students will brainstorm and describe what children's books typically look like and the language they typically use.

As group members decide upon the topic for their children's book, the teacher may recommend that, in order for students to write the book well, they will need to make sure they understand the topic well themselves. To begin the selection process, the students will brainstorm a list of possible suggested topics with which they feel comfortable, perhaps starting with the ideas mentioned at the beginning of this chapter.

As groups complete this initial brainstorming session, student groups will have compiled a list of possible topics. Students will then be invited to bring a children's book for use during the next group meeting on the project.

✳ **FIRST-STORY INTELLECT**

Gathering Information

During this phase of the project, each group will begin *gathering* information for the first-story intellect phase by *reading* at least one or more children's books that group members brought to class. (Refer to Project Learning Log 1 at the end of the chapter.) The group will use these examples to review the parameters of children's books, paying particular attention to the vocabulary used in the books. At this point, roles will be finalized in the group and the production coordinator will tell about the selected partner/teacher and confirm arrangements with that individual. The group will then go back to the list of science book topics, selecting three to discuss in detail. Each member of the group will then *research* each of the topics. Students will use their own textbooks, the classroom library, teachers, and the school library to get more information about the topic.

If chemistry group members, for example, decide to research the shape of the water molecule and the effect of that shape on the properties of water, they might find from their own textbook that the molecule is bent like a boomerang, with the oxygen atom at the bend and the hydrogen atoms at the ends of the arms. Students might learn from their readings that this bending results in a separation of electrical charge so that oxygen is negative and the hydrogens are positive. These sources would tell students that the oxygen in one water molecule and the hydrogens in another molecule attract each other very strongly, just like the opposite poles on a magnet attract. The strong attraction means that molecules in liquid water can really snuggle close to each other; that molecules need to move farther apart when water freezes; and that this is the reason why ice floats. The strong attractions also mean that water has a fairly high melting and boiling point for a molecule its size.

Continuing with the above scenario, the project teacher might suggest to the group that the angle that is formed by the three atoms in a water molecule is like the angle formed by the ears and symbol on a "Mickey Mouse" hat. A member of the group who is familiar with cartoon characters might decide that water is the "Mighty Mouse" of the molecules. This discussion could suggest some character development—specifically, a mouse character—when the group begins to write the book. As the group collects facts and ideas about the topic, the accuracy authority on the team will go back to the textbook, the room library, other members of the class, and the teacher to double-check the facts for scientific accuracy.

Each member of the group will *investigate* reference materials and publications such as *National Geographic, Science Digest, Nature,* or *Discovery* to find photographs that could be used as models to design illustrations for the children's science book and its cover. Members of the chemistry group that is writing on water might find pictures showing icicles, snowflakes or piles of snow, ice cubes floating in a glass of water, water running from a

tap, lakes or rivers, waterfalls, clouds, steam from cooling towers or tea kettles, and pictures of mouse characters. Students may collect photocopies of such pictures or cut them out of their own publications, to be used as ideas for illustrating the book. Also, students may sketch their own ideas for illustrations. The group will give the collection to the illustrator to use in designing the book.

The production coordinator will schedule a time for the whole group to *visit* the partner/teacher at his or her school. During this visit, the teacher will be prepared to show the group some of the books read by primary grade students. The primary school teacher and the group will spend some time compiling a vocabulary list from these books.

If this visit is not practical to arrange, the group may write a letter to the partner/teacher explaining the topic and time lines for the project and asking for a list of words that indicate grade-level appropriate vocabulary for the primary school class. To speed up the transfer of information, the group may give the primary school teacher the telephone number of the production coordinator (or another group member who volunteers for the job) and ask the teacher to telephone the group member with a list of age-appropriate vocabulary. At this point, the group will tell the partner/teacher what topic they have chosen to write about and the date when he or she can expect to see a rough draft of the manuscript.

Members of the group will *interview* teachers at their school, outside of the science department, about some historic, business, literary, or other connections to their topic. A history teacher might tell the group working on a book on water, for example, that high speed and floating icebergs were responsible for the sinking of the *Titanic.* An English teacher might mention that one of his favorite poems about water is "The Rime of the Ancient Mariner." A technology teacher might say that the high boiling point of water and the ability of water to hold heat for a long time make baseboard hot-water radiators a popular system of home heating. Each member of the group will obtain at least three interdisciplinary connections to add to information that might be used in the children's book.

Students can *audiotape* during this stage of the project. For example, the water group could record a variety of water sounds, such as a faucet running or rain falling, to use as background listening during the science lesson.

Students will also *search the Internet* for information about children's books. Some addresses of Web sites that provide good information with links are http://www.gallery-graphics.com/childbks.htm, http://planet-hawaii./com/cybernet/geko/moreinfo.html, and http://www.eli-designs.com/print/books/booksl.html. Some examples of science books for primary school children can be found at http://www.yahooligans.com. Students may also use a search engine such as AltaVista, Yahoo, or WebCrawler to find "juvenile science books."

✳ SECOND-STORY INTELLECT

Focusing on the Goal: A Children's Science Book

The group will begin the second-story intellect phase of this project by *generating* a plan for the children's science book. (Refer to Project Learning Log 2 at the end of the chapter.)

> To finalize their plan, the group members will look over the information they have gathered during the first phase, those items being
>
> - Facts
> - Ideas
> - Interdisciplinary connections
> - Sounds

The team will then go over questions that members have gathered, making decisions on what to include in the book and what to leave out. For example, at this point the water group might decide to start with the composition of the molecule, two hydrogen atoms and one oxygen atom, then go to molecular shape and say that this shape leads to strong attractions much like magnets attracting each other. The group might then go to the closeness of the liquid molecules, their need to move farther apart to form the solid, and the fact that—because of this—ice floats.

Outlining the Book

As the group sets the plan, they will *organize* the book by using a graphic organizer such as a mind map, a standard outline form, or a fishbone. The group will then decide on how to present the story. The water group might remember the singing mice in the movie *Babe,* who moved the story from scene to scene, deciding to have Mighty Water Mouse tell the story of water and its properties. The mouse could be a teacher with a lab coat, Albert Einstein–type hair, and a pointer. A sketch of the mouse pointing to some interesting feature could appear in each picture. With input from teammates, the author of the group will use the graphic organizer to write a *rough draft* of the children's science book.

Illustrating the Book

The illustrator for the group will use his or her copy of the graphic organizer to *sketch* pictures that could go with the text. When the author has finished the rough draft, the accuracy authority will read it, looking at the science facts and double-checking them against the group research. The production coordinator will take the rough draft to the partner/teacher for a

vocabulary check. The production coordinator may seek his or her advice to find age-appropriate words to substitute for any problem vocabulary.

At this point, the group will also name itself as a publishing house and *sketch* an identifying logo that signifies the children's book topic. The water group may call itself "Mighty Molecules, Inc." and use as its trademark a V-shaped ship floating on water with an iceberg looming in the background. This publishing house name and logo can help the group keep its focus as it brainstorms ideas for rewrites and revisions. The group will sketch three possible cover designs for the book and will do a title-page layout.

Developing Prototypes

Each group will use the rough draft that has been checked for science accuracy and age-appropriate vocabulary, the pictures sketched by the illustrator, and the title page and cover designs to develop a *prototype* children's science book. Each group will hold a "paste-up session" during which members cut apart the rough draft to separate the text by pages and paste or tape the text and illustrations together to form a "page dummy."

The production coordinator will have at least three copies of the rough draft for the group to work with so that the text can be combined with different pictures to make several versions of a page. Members of the group will compare the different page layouts and assemble one prototype children's science book that features their favorite layout. The process is much like playing solitaire, with different pages containing the same text but different pictures being shuffled in and out until the group is happy with the overall look of the children's science book. Members of the group will then decide which cover is their favorite and why they like that cover. They will put their favorite page layouts with their favorite cover to assemble a proof copy of the children's science book.

✳ THIRD-STORY INTELLECT

Testing, Showcasing, and Evaluating

Each group or team will move into third-story intellect activities by *trying out* the proof copy of its children's science book. (Refer to Project Learning Log 3 at the end of the chapter.) The team will show its children's science book to another team (the "checker" team) in the class with the two teams going over the text and the illustrations together. Each team will answer questions that the reviewing team might have about the content of its book or the way in which the pictures illustrate the text. Teams will tell each other what they like about the children's science books and what they think needs clarification. The illustrator for a team may choose to *revise* illustrations as the teams discuss them. That way the illustrator can clarify the pictures while other students are there to help develop clear, strong *visualizations* of the book.

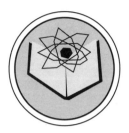

Each team will *test* the vocabulary in its proof copy by having the production coordinator take the children's science book back to the partner/teacher to read and check for age-appropriate vocabulary. The partner/teacher may also suggest revisions in the illustrations to make them more age-appropriate or appealing to young children.

If getting feedback from the partner/teacher isn't a possibility, the group may ask a librarian specializing in children's books, who may be willing to act as a reviewer.

Revising and Assessing

Each group will *evaluate* all the feedback to decide what needs to be re-written. Group members will perform their roles: The author will rewrite the text. The illustrator will produce revised, clarified pictures. The accuracy authority will check science content against recorded facts and will take the text to the project teacher, or perhaps to another science teacher, to double-check content accuracy. Acting as a reviewer, the teacher will tell the group what about the book is accurate, what he or she particularly likes, and what needs clarifying or correcting.

Each team will do a second proof copy of its children's science book. This second prototype will contain the *revised* pictures and *rewritten* and (corrected) text. The group will take this second prototype to the checker group to do a final check for content clarity and age-appropriate vocabulary. The group will do its rewriting with the checker group, librarian reviewer or partner/teacher to get immediate feedback. Each group will end this round of checking with a proof copy of the children's science book that is ready to go to final production.

The group will then assemble the *portfolio* for the project.

This project portfolio will contain the following:

- The brainstormed list of science book topics with the top three indicated.
- The selected topic with the reasons why the group chose the topic.
- The research notes on the selected topic.
- The list indicating age-appropriate vocabulary for the targeted primary grade.
- The graphic organizer or outline for the book.
- The rough drafts of the text and sketches.
- The rough drafts and brainstorm notes for the publishing house name and logo.

- The proof copy of the paste-up with the critique notes from classmates and the partner/teacher (primary grade) or librarian.
- A copy of the presentation version of the science book (This may be a black-and-white photocopy.) and the written feedback from the partner/teacher.

The portfolio will be on display in the school, with the official presentation copy of the book, after the project is completed.

Showcasing the Project

Each group will make a final, presentation copy of its children's science book. The author will type a final version of the children's science book, with correctly spaced text on each page, using word-processing software. The author will print one copy of the text to give to the illustrator for the official illustrations and one back-up copy. The group will meet and the illustrator will sketch the pictures on the pages. The members of the group will color the pictures using brightly colored markers. The group will use a similar technique to produce the cover. The author will provide copy with word-processing software, the illustrator will draw the pictures, and the group will collaborate on coloring the cover. Also, the author will produce a title page and the illustrator will sketch the group logo on the title page. The production coordinator will make a photocopy of the finished pages for each member of the group, then place the original presentation pages in a binder and attach the cover.

At this point, the group will take the assembled children's science book to the partner/teacher who will *showcase* the book by reading it to his or her students, teaching them a science lesson. The partner/teacher and the children will then provide some feedback for the older students, which he or she will produce in writing. Each of the partner/teacher's students may be prompted to contribute two science facts that the child learned from the book and one idea that the child particularly liked or thought was fun. Each child in the class and the teacher will then sign the feedback. The partner/teacher will contact the production coordinator to tell her that the children's science book and the feedback are ready to be picked up.

As the final presentation step, each group will present its children's science book to the class. The accuracy authority will begin by telling the class what topic the group chose to highlight and why the group chose that topic. Next, the author will read the book title to the class and hold up the book to show the cover picture while he or she explains how it illustrates an important idea from the book. The illustrator will tell the class the team's "publishing company" name and the reasons why the team chose that name.

The illustrator will also show the class the logo and explain how it represents the topic in the book as well as the group itself. The production coordinator will read the text to the class while the accuracy authority holds the children's science book so that members of the class can see the pictures. The author and illustrator will take turns explaining how the pictures illustrate the text. Finally, the accuracy authority will read a few of the partner/teacher's students' comments to the class.

The class will *celebrate* success with the presenting group by giving them an energizing cheer.

Self-Evaluation and Group Evaluation

In addition to using the rubric, students will *self-evaluate* by assessing their learnings and project performances as individuals.

> Students will reflect on the following in their journals:
> - Identify two important techniques you learned about producing books for children and why you consider them important.
> - Identify two facts that you learned about your science topic and tell why these facts are particularly significant for you.
> - Considering how you learned throughout this project—by reading, listening, writing, visualizing, outlining, checking, and by responding to feedback, which type of learning did you find most comfortable? Which did you find the least comfortable? How can you improve that comfort level?

For group evaluation, groups will meet and members will share their journal entries with each other, at their discretion.

> Each group will evaluate its work as a team by completing the following:
> - We believe that our teamwork on this project was (<u>pick one of the following: awesome, competent, erratic, what teamwork</u>) because we . . .
> - If our overall performance in producing our children's science book were a thriller movie, the title would be (<u>create an appropriate title such as *Everest Conquered!* or *Escape from the Black Hole*</u>) because we . . .

As a closure activity, each group will *celebrate* at the end this session by giving itself a round of applause and high fives.

Project Evaluation Rubric
Chapter 9: Writing a Children's Science Book

Performance / Criteria	0	1	2	3
Appearance of book cover	Covers are unacceptable: messy; poor printing; careless illustrations	Three or four spelling mistakes; poorly spaced printing; minimal illustrations	No spelling mistakes; one or two spacing problems; good illustrations	No spelling mistakes or spacing problems; very good illustrations
Illustrations in the book	Illustrations do not coordinate with text; small; poor use of color; four or more pages not illustrated	Illustrations coordinate with text; small; good use of color; only three pages not illustrated	Illustrations coordinate with text; large and colorful; only one or two pages not illustrated	Illustrations coordinate with text; large and colorful; all pages illustrated
Text (copy) in the book	Five or more content or typographical errors; "rough draft" appearance	Three or four content or typographical errors; clean copy	One or two content or typographical errors; clean copy	No errors of any kind; clean copy
Transitions between ideas/concepts presented in the book	No transitions between ideas/concepts	Three or four awkward breaks between ideas/concepts	One or two awkward breaks between ideas/concepts	Good use of transitions; text flows from one idea to the next
Use of age-appropriate vocabulary in book	Five or more vocabulary problems as noted by primary school reviewer (partner/teacher)	Three or four vocabulary problems as noted by primary school reviewer (partner/teacher)	One or two vocabulary problems as noted by primary school reviewer (partner/teacher)	No vocabulary problems noted by primary school reviewer (partner/teacher)

Project Learning Log 1

✳ **First-Story Intellect: Gathering Information**

Describe what you did to gather information.

• **Read**

. . . .

. . . .

. . . .

• **Visited**

. . . .

. . . .

. . . .

• **Researched**

. . . .

. . . .

. . . .

• **Interviewed**

. . . .

. . . .

. . . .

• **Surfed the 'Net**

. . . .

. . . .

. . . .

• **And . . .**

. . . .

. . . .

Project Learning Log 2

✸ **Second-Story Intellect: Processing Information**

Describe what you did to process information.

- **Sketched**

....

....

....

- **Analyzed**

....

....

....

- **Calculated/Graphed**

....

....

....

- **Developed Prototypes**

....

....

....

- **Drew**

....

....

....

- **And . . .**

....

....

Project Learning Log 3

✳ **Third-Story Intellect: Applying Information**

Describe what you did to apply information.

- **Tried/Tested**

....
....
....

- **Evaluated**

....
....
....

- **Revised**

....
....
....

- **Repeated the Cycle**

....
....
....

- **Showcased**

....
....
....

- **And . . .**

....
....

SkyLight Training and Publishing, Inc.

Blackline Masters

The following blackline masters will prove useful when implementing project learning as a curriculum model. The first blackline is a conceptualization of the three-story intellect for the multiple intelligences classroom. The other blacklines provide specific information about each of the three stories: gathering, processing, and applying.

The Three-Story Intellect with Multiple Intelligences

3 APPLYING

Verbal: using metaphors, similes, analogies, puns, plays on words

Visual: visualizing, imagining, dreaming, envisioning, symbolizing

Logical: evaluating, judging, refining, creating analogies, reasoning, critiquing

Musical: composing, improvising, critiquing, performing, conducting

Bodily: constructing, dramatizing, peforming, experimenting, sculpting

Interpersonal: debating, compromising, mediating, arbitrating,

Intrapersonal: meditating, intuiting, innovating, inventing, creating

Naturalist: forecasting, predicting, interrelating, synthesizing, categorizing

PROCESSING 2 Crystallize Ideas

Verbal: paraphrasing, essay writing, labeling, reporting, organizing

Visual: sketching, mapping, diagramming, illustrating, cartooning

Logical: graphing, comparing, classifying, ranking, analyzing, coding

Musical: playing, selecting, singing, responding to music

Bodily: rehearsing, studying, experimenting, investigating

Interpersonal: expressing, telling/retelling, arguing, discussing

Intrapersonal: studying, self-assessing, interpreting, processing

GATHERING 1 Research Project

Verbal: questioning, reading, listing, telling, writing, finding, listening, documenting

Visual: viewing, observing, seeing, describing, showing

Logical: recording, collecting, logging, documenting

Musical: listening, gathering, audiotaping, attending concerts

Bodily: preparing, exploring, investigating, interviewing

Interpersonal: interacting, teaming, interviewing, affirming

Intrapersonal: reflecting, expressing, reacting, journaling

SkyLight Training and Publishing, Inc.

Gathering Ideas:
Researching the Project

Reading for background information

Researching and taking notes

Building a reference list

Interviewing experts

Viewing films and videos

Developing an outline

Talking with peers

Surfing the Internet

Checking and double-checking sources

Visiting sites

Gathering charts, maps, illustrations

Processing Information: Crystallizing Ideas

Brainstorming ideas

Analyzing data

Charting information

Drawing and sketching models

Drafting ideas

Developing prototypes

Filling in missing information

Visualizing the big picture

Reconciling conflicting data

Finding a focus

Assigning a theme

Creating a metaphor

Looking for patterns

Seeking connections

Playing with ideas

Finding materials

SkyLight Training and Publishing, Inc.

Applying Ideas:
Trying and Testing

Model building

Construction

Assembling

Synthesizing ideas

Rethinking or reconceptualizing

Finishing touches

Decorative details

Evaluative testing

Peer review

Self-assessment

Evaluation against criteria

Expert review

Final submittals

Celebrations

Bibliography

Ambrose, Stephen. *Undaunted Courage*. New York, NY: Simon and Schuster, 1996.

Armstrong, Thomas. *Seven Kinds of Smart: Discovering and Using Your Natural Intelligences*. New York, NY: Penguin, 1993.

———. *Multiple Intelligences in the Classroom*. Alexandria, VA: Association for Supervision and Curriculum Development, 1994.

Barton, Lois, ed. *One Woman's West: Recollections of the Oregon Trail and Settling the Northwest Country by Martha Gay Masterson, 1838–1916*. 2d ed. Eugene, OR: Spencer Butte Press, 1990.

Bellanca, James. *Catch Them Thinking: A Handbook of Classroom Strategies*. Palatine, IL: IRI/SkyLight Training and Publishing, 1986.

———. *The Cooperative Think Tank*. Palatine, IL: IRI/SkyLight Training and Publishing, 1990.

Bellanca, James, and Robin Fogarty. *Blueprints for Thinking in the Cooperative Classroom*. Palatine, IL: IRI/SkyLight Publishing, 1990.

Bill Nye, the Science Guy: Simple Machines. Burbank, CA: Walt Disney Home Video, 1996, videotape.

Blackburn, Graham. *Furniture by Design: Design, Construction and Technique*. New York, NY: Lyons and Burford, 1997.

Boring, Mel, and Linda Garrow. *Birds, Nests and Eggs*. Minocqua, WI: NorthWord Press, 1996.

Brockman, C. Frank. *Trees of North America*. Racine, WI: Western Publishing, 1968.

Burke, Kay. *The Mindful School: How to Assess Authentic Learning*. Palatine, IL: IRI/SkyLight Training and Publishing, 1994.

Catherall, Ed. *Exploring Uses of Energy*. Austin, TX: Steck-Vaughn, 1991.

Chapman, Carolyn. *If the Shoe Fits . . .: How to Develop Multiple Intelligences in the Classroom*. Palatine, IL: IRI/SkyLight Training and Publishing, 1993.

Chitty Chitty Bang Bang. Los Angeles, CA: MGM/United Artists, 1968.

Costa, Arthur L. *The School as a Home for the Mind.* Palatine, IL: IRI/SkyLight Training and Publishing, 1991.

Crocker, Mark, and Nicola Barber. *The Body Atlas.* New York, NY: Oxford University Press Children's Books, 1994.

Dictionary of International Biography. Cambridge, England: International Biographical Centre, 1995.

Eisen, David. *Fun with Architecture.* New York, NY: HarperCollins, 1992.

Farrand, John Jr. *Eastern Birds: An Audubon Handbook.* New York, NY: McGraw-Hill, 1988.

Figtree, Dale. *Eat Smart: A Guide to Good Health for Kids.* Tulsa, OK: Winchester Press, 1997.

Flexner, James Thomas. *Washington: The Indispensable Man.* Boston, MA: Little, Brown, 1974.

Fogarty, Robin. *Problem-Based Learning and Other Curriculum Models for the Multiple Intelligences Classroom*: Arlington Heights, IL: IRI/ SkyLight Training and Publishing, 1997.

Fogarty, Robin, and James Bellanca. *Patterns for Thinking—Patterns for Transfer.* Palatine, IL: IRI/SkyLight Publishing, 1993.

Frimodig, David M., comp. *A Most Superior Land.* Lansing, MI: Two Peninsula Press, 1983.

Gardner, Howard. *Frames of Mind: The Theory of Multiple Intelligences.* New York, NY: Basic Books, 1983.

———. *Multiple Intelligences: The Theory in Practice.* New York, NY: Basic Books, 1993.

Gowans, Alan. *Styles and Types of North American Architecture.* New York, NY: HarperCollins, 1992.

Holling, Holling Clancy. *Paddle-to-the-Sea.* New York, NY: Houghton Mifflin, 1941.

Jennings, Terry J. *Forces and Machines.* Austin, TX: Raintree/Steck-Vaughn, 1995.

Johnson, David W., Roger T. Johnson, and Edythe Johnson Holubec. *Cooperation in the Classroom.* Edina, MN: Interaction Book, 1988.

Johnson, Pamela, ed. *Iowa: A Celebration of Land, People and Purpose.* Des Moines, IA: Meredith Publishing, 1995.

Kalman, Bobbie, and Glen Oates. *Birds at My Feeder.* New York, NY: Crabtree Publishing, 1988.

Lazear, David. *Seven Ways of Knowing: Teaching for Multiple Intelligences.* Palatine, IL: Skylight Publishing, 1991.

SkyLight Training and Publishing, Inc.

————. *Seven Ways of Teaching: The Artistry of Teaching with Multiple Intelligences*. Palatine, IL: IRI/Skylight Training and Publishing, 1991.

Leopold, Aldo. *A Sand County Almanac and Sketches Here and There*. New York, NY: Oxford University Press, 1949.

Martz, Sandra, ed. *When I Am an Old Woman I Shall Wear Purple*. Watsonville, CA: Papier-Mache Press, 1991.

McGraw-Hill Encyclopedia of Science and Technology. New York, NY: McGraw-Hill, 1997.

McGraw-Hill Encyclopedia of World Biography. New York, NY: McGraw-Hill, 1975.

McNally, Andrew. *Rand McNally Road Atlas: United States, Canada, Mexico*. Skokie, IL: Rand, McNally, 1997.

Michigan Magic. Escanaba, MI: Michigan Magic Productions, 1990, videotape.

Milne, A. A. *Winnie the Pooh*. New York, NY: E. P. Dutton, 1927.

Murnane, Richard J., and Frank Levy. *Teaching the New Basic Skills: Principles for Educating Children to Thrive in a Changing Economy*. New York, NY: Free Press, 1996.

The Oregon Coast: An Adventure Awaits. Portland, OR: EMA Video, 1993, videotape.

Peterson, Roger Tory. *A Field Guide to the Birds of Eastern and Central North America*. Boston, MA: Houghton Mifflin, 1980.

Peterson, Roger Tory, and Margaret McKenny. *A Field Guide to Wildflowers of Northeastern and Northcentral America*. Boston, MA: Houghton Mifflin, 1968.

Smith, Page. *Old Age Is Another Country: A Traveler's Guide*. Freedom, CA: Crossing Press, 1995.

Stokes, Lillian, and Donald W. Stokes. *The Birdfeeder Book*. Boston, MA: Little, Brown, 1987.

Toys, Games, and Furniture. Cincinnati, OH: Reader's Digest, 1995.

Tribole, Evelyn. *Eating on the Run*. Champaign, IL: Leisure Press, 1991.

Trivizas, Eugene, and Helen Oxenbury (Illustrator). *The Three Little Wolves and the Big Bad Pig*. New York, NY: Macmillan, 1993.

Wells, Malcolm. *Build a Better Birdhouse (or Feeder)*. Minocqua, WI: Willow Creek Press, 1996.

Wells, Robert E. *How Do You Lift a Lion?* Morton Grove, IL: Albert Whitman, 1996.

Index

SkyLight Training and Publishing, Inc.

SkyLight Training and Publishing, Inc.

Notes

Notes

SkyLight

Learn from Our Books *and* from Our Authors!

Bring Our Authors/Trainers to Your District

Professional development is a process, not an event. With SkyLight Training and Publishing, Inc., that process begins with a school's need to increase student achievement. Our cadre of dynamic, classroom-experienced consultants is dedicated to helping you foster systemic change in your school or district.

Skylight specializes in three professional development areas.

Specialty # **1**

Best Practices

Consultants help teachers make immediate use of new ideas by modeling the research-based "best practices" that have resulted in improved student performance. Whether working with curriculum, instructional strategies, restructuring or assessment techniques, the consultants assist teachers to transfer effective instructional models to the classroom.

Specialty # **2**

Making the Innovations Last

Consultants help set up the support systems (peer sharing, collegial teams, action research projects) that make their innovations part of everyday practice in a systemic improvement for your school or district.

Specialty # **3**

How to Assess the Results

Consultants prepare your school leaders to assess teacher growth, encourage teacher growth, measure student achievement, and evaluate program success.

SkyLight provides educational seminars, on-site professional development at your school or district, graduate courses, research-based publications, interactive videos and training materials, and online resources through our web site (www.iriskylight.com).

The SkyLight team works with you to foster and motivate teacher growth, increase student achievement, and meet the goals and standards of your school or district. **Contact us and begin a process toward long-term results.**

SkyLight

TRAINING AND PUBLISHING, INC.
2626 S. Clearbrook Dr., Arlington Heights, IL 60005
800-348-4474 • 847-290-6600 • FAX 847-290-6609
http://www.iriskylight.com

There are

one-story intellects,

two-story intellects, and three-story

intellects with skylights. All fact collectors, who

have no aim beyond their facts, are one-story men. Two-story men

compare, reason, generalize, using the labors of the fact collectors as

well as their own. Three-story men idealize, imagine,

predict—their best illumination comes from

above, through the skylight.

—*Oliver Wendell*

Holmes

SkyLight

TRAINING AND PUBLISHING, INC.